Seven Step Business Plan

Seven Step Business Plan

SHEILA HOLM

FOREWORD BY
KEN BLANCHARD

PELICAN PUBLISHING COMPANY
GRETNA 2007

The word "Pelican" and the depiction of a pelican
are trademarks of Pelican Publishing Company, Inc.,
and are registered in the U.S. Patent and Trademark Office.

Library of Congress Cataloging-in-Publication Data

Holm, Sheila.
  Seven step business plan / Sheila Holm ; foreword by Ken
Blanchard.
      p. cm.
  ISBN 978-1-58980-471-5 (hardcover : alk. paper)
  1. Business planning. I. Title.
  HD30.28.H674 2007
  658.4'01—dc22

                                    2006100010

Printed in the United States of America
Published by Pelican Publishing Company, Inc.
1000 Burmaster Street, Gretna, Louisiana 70053

To my mother and father, Irvin and Clarice Holm, for being excellent lifetime examples of remaining grounded, operating in integrity while expressing the entrepreneurial spirit in the face of any and all circumstances, and persevering through each new crisis with grace.

To my ancestors, both Norwegian and Scottish, for becoming entrepreneurs in each community, establishing businesses and community structures that stand as excellent examples of my generational legacy to this day, and for proceeding in spite of the obstacles, confirming it is okay to take risks!

To Ken Blanchard, for being a superb example of leadership, for providing a leadership program that supports people in paving their own way in business, for always keeping the planning process simple and concise, and for making mentorship an art that deeply touches millions of individuals and positively affects their lives and businesses!

To all of the people and businesses who have challenged my choices and decisions, for committing time and effort to making me become a better person in business today than I was yesterday. Thanks!

Contents

Foreword

In *The One Minute Manager,* Spencer Johnson and I argued that the first secret to effective management is One Minute Goal Setting. All good performance starts with clear goals. If you do not know where you are going, any road will get you there.

Sheila Holm heard me deliver that message more than twenty years ago at the first meeting of the SONY Management Club in San Diego. It so affected her that she became interested in the whole area of business planning. She learned early that failing to plan results in a business actually planning to fail. That is why she wrote *Seven Step Business Plan.*

Holm offers a practical, step-by-step guide that provides every person in business—from one owner to a partnership, department, or division of a major corporation—with a one-page business plan simply by filling in the blanks. *Seven Step Business Plan* can be easily adapted for any business in any industry and it can be easily updated on a weekly or monthly basis.

As far as I am concerned, *Seven Step Business Plan* is the first and only book to provide a simple format for every business to be able to prepare and update their business plan. Enjoy this book and recognize that it can make a difference in how successful your business can be.

Remember, all good performance starts with clear goals and direction. Thanks, Sheila, for providing this to make any business more successful.

KEN BLANCHARD

Preface

Before preparing this book for you, I cycled and recycled clients to every bookstore to work through every business-planning book option. They purchased many books; however, they still wanted more help.

To make it easy and affordable for more business owners to receive help, I started conducting a series of seminars to help owners and their management teams develop their business plans within a seven-step format based upon their dreams and goals. The seminar outline rapidly developed into a seven-step, one-page form for quick and easy review while updating the business plan according to each change and adjustment to the goals.

Ownership of the business plan adds value to the bottom line of the business!

Seven Step Business Plan removes the learning-curve requirement. I know you can increase the productivity and profitability of your business when you write your own business plan. I have watched it happen, repeatedly, as clients learn these steps. You are the reason why I developed the simple "fill in the blanks" form to establish the Seven Step Business Plan.

The ability to personally adjust the business plan results in a boost to the profitability of the business. The seven-step, one-page plan remains "in view" and "up to date" with frequent input from the staff. This is one reason why the one-page format became the core element of the only

entrepreneurial program provided for the federal contract during the conversion of the defense and aerospace
industry technology into commercial businesses in the
late 1990s.

Their success stories, and each client story, are now past
history. It is your turn to fill in the blanks with your future
goals and proceed based upon your seven steps for your own
Seven Step Business Plan.

So, Where Do You Begin?

The bottom line, since business owners are bottom-line
thinkers: You do not have time to figure out a business-planning process or theory and then figure out how to write your
thoughts into a succinct business plan. Your long-term
dream, or new business idea, has been percolating for a
while and by now it has finally bubbled over, causing you to
purchase this book.

You and your support team can easily fill in the blanks of
the Seven Step Business Plan and develop the plan together,
so each member of the team will share in the ownership of
the goals with everyone accountable for their participation
in the business. Your plan then becomes an active part of
each business planning session, and the plan can easily be
updated during any meeting or whenever a member of the
team sets new goals for any part of the business.

Be sure to share your successes based upon using the
Seven Step Business Plan. Looking forward to the day when
I will be reading your success story—soon, very soon!

Here's to you, and to your *Seven Step Business Plan* results
and increased profits!

SHEILA HOLM

Introduction:
Begin the Planning Process

Congratulations! You are hired. You are the best person I could find to write your business plan! With notepad and pen in hand, you are ready to begin.

Begin Writing the Plan Today, One Step at a Time

Procrastination is expensive. Avoid that step. Find a full pad of blank paper and a good pen or a stack of pens or pencils. Then, find a comfortable chair and a good place with good light to read and immediately write down the gems you think about as you continue to turn the pages.

Whether you have not yet written a plan, you have paid a consultant to write a plan, or you have proceeded with your business idea before writing a plan, you are absolutely in the majority. But the truth is that no other owner, director, or team leader can articulate your business idea better than you can. If you circled the globe and interviewed the best of the best, you would not find a single person who knows your business ideas and dreams better than you do, and they would not be able to articulate the ideas until you provided the facts. This is why I congratulate you on your decision. You have taken a positive step toward owning your business plan for your team, your division, or your company. Bravo!

Planning is the key to success and profitability.
The old saying is true:
"failing to plan = planning to fail."

How will you find the time to sit down and write? Well, there is a little secret about time. I am going to share it since you have agreed to take on the challenge of writing your business plan—Seven Step at a time.

The problem with our time and the planning process is this: we forget to set aside time to plan. If we do not find the time to plan, we will proceed without a structured plan.

To begin, we have to start from a different perspective regarding our daily calendar. When we use typical calendars, we become trained to believe the important hours are the hours on the calendar. That lie puts our lives into a spin. The spin increases in size and speed as each day passes. Is this sounding like your daily life yet? The spin is difficult to recover from until we realize we are in a spin and we have the power to stop the spin, sit down, and plan our lives, our daily time. Then, we can begin to see how we are spending our time and how we can improve upon the daily schedule and our planning processes.

Everything worth doing requires time. Every task in daily life requires time. Let's get real: even finding the time to think about our time requires time. The good news is that every memory is created from the time we spend contributing to the task of the moment. When we contribute time toward our goals, our time expands, for we become conscious of the ways we are spending our moments. Thus we begin the contribution cycle of time—every bit of time we contribute provides us with more time to ultimately contribute to the cycle—by recognizing the gift of the "extra" time each day.

Most people do not set aside time to plan for specific goals, and that is why they have the same goals on their list the next time you talk to them. Your choice requires a shift in focus for life to be different. Focusing on your accomplishments and taking the steps required for the next phase of your business are exactly what will carry you to your next set of goals. It is a process.

To do this, start by finding time for yourself. If you are having difficulty, do not worry. This is where we all start since we have been using the "short day" calendars for so long. Over time, we have lost our place within our own schedule! It will help you to shift the focus to yourself by pretending you are meeting someone else for coffee, so go ahead and put my name on your calendar. Then take a pad of paper and this book along with you as you give yourself the time to meet with me and work on your plans. Surprise! You will not be alone. I have structured the book so that I will be with you each step of the way.

If you do not think you even have time for a cup of coffee during the week yet, arrange your planning time on Saturday for right now. Together, we will work toward your goals, making each moment count, and setting you on your way to developing your own contribution cycle of time. OK?

The Goal

Increase the planning minutes "set aside" every day of the week. Whether you start by setting aside 10 percent of the day, 2.4 hours, or you start at 5 percent and increase to 10 percent, at least start the process! As you continue to set new goals, you will fill your time with new assignments, since this process is a layered process. What is important in this very moment?

Bottom Line

Find some time to give to yourself, even if you only find twenty minutes today. As much time as you can give me today, thanks, in advance!

1
Structure

Immediately, in your own words, begin writing a statement about "how it is around here" according to how you are going to proceed with your business. Sad but true, many owners, even after they open the doors and operate their business, proceed without a clear statement about their business: how it will meet the needs of customers or how their business relates to the industry. Their dreams and goals are not in writing or in focus yet.

Your "Business According to You" Begins Right Now

Clarity is helpful and it has a positive impact upon your bottom line. So, do you want more profit? Then, gain clarity. Want more clarity? Then, schedule a little more time to walk/work through the planning process with me.

Seven Phases of the Business Process

Business develops in phases, so it is important to begin the planning process by identifying the part of one or more phases, or stages of development, of the business process your business represents. Your business may be at a point where you want to add a phase of the business to your existing plans or it may be an idea that you want to sell to someone else. You may want to purchase a developed product in order to market and distribute it, or you may be starting a business that will include all phases of the business process.

This step is a major decision point since it will match your expertise and passion with the type of business you should pursue. So, take a moment to get comfortable and get a firm picture in your head of yourself as the owner of the concept or product in one or more of the key phases of the business.

1. Idea
Invention or creation, up to or including research for development or production. Ideas are often fostered to the point where they can be sold for development.

Example: A client just wanted a plan regarding his idea. He did not want to run the business, but he had an idea that was not in the marketplace and he knew it would be profitable. Therefore, we developed a business plan and highlighted the fact that the idea could be "franchised" (duplicated) in various parts of the country and around the globe. With the clear idea defined within a feasible business plan, he sold his plan to a publicly listed corporation for a few million dollars. He also offered to remain available as a consultant, which resulted in additional, significant income for the next five years.

2. Development
From research and development to defining the structure.

Development of the idea can result in successfully selling the structure of the business without opening a production or business location.

Example: A client had a great design concept. She planned to sell the design as a logo on various products, i.e., T-shirts, mugs, etc. After analyzing the idea, she realized she would be paying for the products, processing, and shipping before being paid, and she would be responsible for paying for all marketing costs. She finally agreed it would be best to license the logo design so various products could be sold with her logo through companies that are already known in the marketplace, and they would provide the products to their established client base. She receives a residual income for each sale without showing up for work or becoming responsible for expenses!

3. Location

The type of office, retail, or business building space you will require in order to house your business. Production, manufacturing, sales, distribution, repair, retail, and wholesale needs must be considered as well as whether the business will be launched locally or internationally.

Example: A client decided to use the home garage to begin the business. However, as soon as the client realized the large volume of products that would have to be shipped daily from his small garage to cover the expenses, he changed the business location.

Example: A client was using the dining room and garage to operate a trophy business. The inconvenience of running such an enterprise out of his home nearly cost the man his twenty-year marriage. During a family meeting, his two sons suggested opening a certificate business. Within ninety days, the two sons were able to secure a leased location that they used to house the trophy and certificate business. The sons paid for their college education through the profits from this business, and their father was able to save his marriage.

4. Production

Identification of products and services for the customer base leads many businesses to specialize only in manufacturing or creating the product. They do not invent or develop the business idea and they do not distribute the product.

Example: A client decided to produce the products and discontinue the marketing, billing, and shipping phases of the business by using a successful and well-placed fulfillment corporation. Profit margin of the business doubled within ninety days!

5. Marketing & Sales

Defining market niche and developing a sales strategy.

Some businesses only market or sell products invented and produced by other businesses.

Example: A client was excellent in marketing products and services. His mistake was in trying to develop and produce these products and services, which kept the business in the "hobby" level of income after two years of extensive effort. Once he realized that he needed to establish a strategic alliance with a production company to produce his products, the marketing figures steadily increased with a significant profit margin established within six months. This status allowed him to stop having a hobby he called a business, stop working as an employee, and flourish as an entrepreneur and business owner.

6. Distribution

From point of sale through a distribution center to a retail outlet or direct to the customer. Some businesses are developed to only distribute products to the next phase of development or to the consumer after the products are sold.

Example: A client met me after she gave up a business that provided her with $5,000 profit per month. Why? She was killing herself by doing everything. She hated the packaging and mailing phase of the business because it "robbed" her of the quality life she enjoyed before starting the business. Within thirty days of our initial meeting, she reactivated the business after establishing a strategic alliance with a fulfillment house to handle the orders, distribute the products to the customers, and resolve the returns. Her profit margin increased significantly since sales were not restrained.

Example: A client insisted he wanted to establish a parts business for recreational vehicles. At any time a part is needed, wherever the customer is located, the part would be provided within minutes rather than hours. Clearly, he recognized a need. It was evident; he had experienced a wait of hours and even days for a part after his recreational vehicle needed repairs.

Bottom Line: It is not practical to provide this level of response and parts distribution. He would have to carry an extensive inventory for every recreational vehicle, pay employees to staff the phones at all hours of the day and night, and then arrange for delivery to any destination, since the business was being established to provide parts within minutes . . . wherever the customer is located.

7. Repairs or Redevelopment

Returns, warranty work, repair, restructure, and recycle. Some businesses are developed only to repair, warranty, or recycle products.

Example: A client was living like the washing-machine repairman in the ads: nobody was calling. He did not have another option for income. Since he represented a sturdy product base, the calls for repair were few and far between. We met after he heard I was a "marketing guru." He trusted I could "guru" him to a profitable business level by shaking the bushes to find more customers.

Bottom Line: He did need more customers. However, he needed additional revenue streams. As soon as we identified additional products and services for his same client base, his business began to flourish.

My Mistake

When I started my first business, I took on the responsibility for all phases of the business. I trusted I could save money, and I thought every business owner takes on all aspects of the business until other options are affordable. However, this meant I also took on the costs for each of the phases and I personally carried all the expenses until I obtained the first payments from our customers. This is a tough way to establish the structure of the business and then to do business. I do not recommend it!

Be cautious. The business development phase can become so exciting, you can easily become isolated from the business community and lose perspective. I was so busy finding an office space to lease and designing the layout while hiring the staff and doing everything to save costs I did not realize invoices were not developed or in the mail the first weeks of the business. I was spread so thin while running on pure adrenaline and managing everything, I did not have time to market the business. I went from marketing guru to exhausted entrepreneur without a break.

Marketing is my area of expertise, so it became my blind spot. Marketing is a phase of business development that is second nature to me, so much so that I did not even realize I had dropped the ball. Since I was the owner, I was the person who needed to see the big picture and keep the business goals in perspective for everyone involved with the business.

Bottom Line: Remain objective and practical while you define your business and what you know you can accomplish.

> *Only you can define specifically how*
> *your business will be structured.*
> *Only you can state how your business*
> *transactions will be conducted.*

Until you schedule time to plan, to think through your business idea from beginning to end and fill in the blanks, be careful what you choose to be responsible for before you commit your hours and dollars to a business. You may decide that it is more beneficial for you to focus only upon one business phase for your business plan. I have provided a few examples to help you during the thinking process since your decisions are critical and need to be specifically stated within your plan. When this decision is clear and understood by all vendors and companies that have formed strategic alliances with you, the flow of the business will begin.

"How it is around here" is absolutely up to you!

Whether you decide that your business idea will encompass one or more of the phases of the business or that you will take on all phases of the business, a winning business strategy is to establish key strategic alliances within the community, local to international, and within the industry. You want your business to become the business that is significant within the industry. Where you are positioned, both the location and your standing within the industry, will speak volumes to your customers. Are you launching a business that is in the early stages of the industry? Will your business influence the industry in a unique way? Do you have a business that will attract customers in a new or larger market niche? Express your passion about your idea when you describe your business so the plan confirms how and why your business will make a difference in the industry.

Why is this so important? Many businesses fail within the first few months of establishing or expanding the idea due to the costs of carrying the new idea forward until it is profitable. In fact, the majority of businesses that proceed through the business loan process, even after they are thoroughly "planned," still fail within the first year of business. When the business is not able to consistently cover the ongoing expenses of the business or pay for the supplies or services required to proceed with the business each month, the business fails.

WARNING: Your business idea is still "on the drawing board." Create it your way!

Too often, clients get excited about the strategic alliances that immediately come to mind, and they begin negotiating deals before all the information is available. It is too early in the planning phase to begin committing to other business-es. At this time, it is more important to make a list of the potential businesses you can contact. Keep adding to the list as we continue through the planning process. This is a good time in the process to pick up a pad of paper and pen and go for a walk. Often, ideas come to mind when you pull away from the process.

You will have enough time to put your plan together—to adjust the business idea and define the business structure—before you commit to any agreements with businesses in the other phases of the business process or potential vendors you will enter into a strategic alliance with. This step is critical, since all of the options need to be considered as you review your business type and industry.

Business Type: Defining the Business

When I wrote my first business plan, I tried to follow the outline supplied by my bank. The outline was developed to help owners applying for a small business loan. At first glance, it seemed like a very simple outline. However, every term they used required a level of understanding that I did not possess. One term that I misunderstand was "business type." I thought business type and industry were the same—one term fits both—however, the two terms are very different. Business type describes your specific business phase and purpose as well as the services you provide within an industry. Some businesses are comprised of all phases and are simple to define since they fit into a specific industry, while some businesses are specific to only one part of the business within an industry or are part of numerous industries. Your industry is the specific branch of manufacture or trade in which your business is involved.

Business Type	Industry	Business Phase
Truck or Car	*Automotive*	
Design	Automotive	Development
Manufacturing	Automotive	Production
Sales	Automotive	Marketing & Sales
Used Sales	Automotive	Sales/ Redevelopment
Mechanic, Diesel	Automotive, Diesel	Repair
Mechanic, Gas	Automotive, Gasoline	Repair
Mechanic, Transmission	Automotive	Repair
Mechanic, Brakes	Automotive	Repair

This chart represents a small segment of the various business types within one given industry: automotive. These examples are provided simply to begin the process of recognizing how specific your business type may be within your specific industry. The automobile manufacturer does not sell the vehicle, which seems easy to figure out since the business type and industry identification process is easily recognized. However, as you review your notes, your business idea may not be as easy to determine.

Your Exact Phase of the Business

After you have defined your business type and determined your industry, you need to clarify the phase(s) that define your business process within the industry. As you read the questions below, keep the following points in mind:

- Your specific business type is the exact business you are going to operate within the industry.
- The business description is vital, and each word of your business description is important.

1. What is your product or service?
2. Who will benefit from the business?
   a. Who needs your products and services?
   b. Will the customer come to your place of business?
   c. What is the customer's income level? What is their ability to pay for your products/services?
   d. How will you reach customers who want information?
   e. How will they benefit from and purchase your products and services?
   f. What can your customer expect from your business?
3. Why does your business exist?
   a. What will your business accomplish in your business community, whether local, national, or international?
   b. Are you establishing a business that will provide a product or service to a mass market or will consumers place custom orders?
4. Where should your business exist?
   a. Is your business community your local town, region, state or province, nation, or part of the international marketplace?
   b. Where will the business be located? Where will transactions take place?

    c. Will you be selling from a wholesale or retail location?
    d. Will you be establishing one or more locations?
    e. Will you be setting up a business within one region or on the Internet?
    f. Will the customer come to your place of business?
    g. Will you arrange delivery or involve a vendor to fulfill the orders?
5. How will your business transactions be conducted?
    a. Will the customer come to your place of business?
    b. Will you be selling from a wholesale or retail location?
6. When will your business be "in business" for the customers?
    a. Will you be open seven days a week?
    b. Will you be closed on weekends and holidays?

Answering these questions is a big step toward developing a successful plan!

You will have additional opportunities to answer the questions about your business type and phase as you define your business within your industry and when you prepare the 30-second commercial for your business. Right now, it is important to take a few moments and begin to see how your business idea is taking shape and becoming part of an overall business structure, even if it is only taking shape in your mind and not appearing on a piece of paper, yet.

Industry: Identifying Your Position

It is important to begin the process of identifying your industry and the position of your business within the industry. Though you will further define the placement of your business in chapter 2, right now, you are in the initial stages of defining the business. Think about how you would describe:

• Your business type within the industry

- The phase(s) of the industry your business will be involved in
- Strategic alliances with businesses in other phase(s) of the industry
- Businesses within your business type, in other communities, and how they are establishing and marketing the business within the industry and to the customers

1. Why is your business a key business within the industry?
   a. What do you bring to the industry?
   b. What does your business idea bring to the industry?
   c. What will you bring to the industry that is not available at this time?
2. How does your business serve needs within the industry?
3. How is your business unique from other businesses within the industry?
4. Where is your business positioned within the industry?
5. Who is served?
6. What are the benefits of your business for the industry/customers?
7. When will your business take the rightful place within the industry?

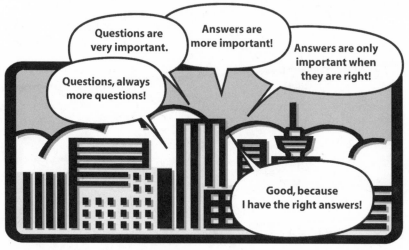

Legal Structure:
Determining Organizational Options

When you clearly determine your organizational options, you define the ownership, legal, and tax structures and define the financial plan for your business. Following is a list of key points to consider when establishing the organization of your business.

1. Name of Your Business

If you will be using a business name other than your name, a fictitious business name, a DBA, or "doing business as" document, needs to be completed and filed before you proceed. When you file the paperwork, you will be asked to provide the business title. The recording office for business filings in your area will have a listing of all business titles already in use. It is important to review the list and be sure you will have "clear title" rights to the business name you want to use.

Establish the business location as well. The address for the business needs to be supplied when you file any paperwork. This information becomes public record and is easily accessible to marketing companies, so a post office box is recommended. This step will keep the mailing address separate from your business's physical location.

Be sure to decide upon the name of your business and your mailing address before you proceed. If you make changes to this information in a week or a month, you will have to repeat every step of filing the local and state or province paperwork for the business.

How Is Your Business
Going to Be Established?
According to You! Make it a Golden Rule!

2. An Independent Contractor or Sole-Proprietor-Based Business

If you are the only owner, you absolutely want to look at the tax options as a sole-proprietor or the owner of a corporation. The first step is to inventory and distinguish your personal assets from your business assets and establish a trust, personal or family, for your personal assets and accounts.

3. Financial or Managing Partners

Thinking about establishing a partnership? My best recommendation is to remove the word "partner" from your vocabulary. The excitement you feel while establishing a business with a partner is intoxicating in the early development phases, but entering into a business agreement with a partner is identical to "marrying" the partner. I have been called in too often to help with the breakup, or "divorce phase," of the partnership—without a community property statute to help unravel the issues or split the equipment/assets/profits.

If you have not entered into a specific contractual agreement that clearly defines all the buyout and sales options and how the discrepancies of the records will be handled, then the best option is to arrange for a limited liability company or corporation structure. This structure will keep you independent from other partners regarding your level of liability for actions, finances, and decisions.

In either scenario, be sure to define as many plans and decisions in writing as possible. The best way to know what another person interested in being involved is thinking about the business is to immediately get everything being considered, discussed, or agreed to in writing. Then, review each line and have all parties initial each line of the document. A good option: Ask the person to *independently* complete the Seven Step Business Plan form, then compare notes and determine if you are headed toward the same business goals.

It is important to prepare the draft copy of each step of

the Seven Step Business Plan. Review the prior steps as you further define your business idea into a concise and succinct plan before you schedule an appointment with a business attorney and a CPA to review the content. Your initial appointment will be free, so be 100 percent ready to review all your questions and concerns before the time clock starts and you make a decision regarding which attorney and CPA you will allow to advise you as you proceed.

4. A Corporation Structure

It is critical to establish a limited liability company or corporation when more than one owner will be involved. Most businesses established as partnerships have changed to limited liability companies or corporations, so the liability is limited to the exposure of each, specific owner.

Before you establish the corporation, it is important to be aware of the various options of the corporation financial and business structure available within your state or province, based upon your regional or national laws. Establishing a corporation can be beneficial, as the tax structure is different for the different types of corporations, "for profit" C or S, etc., or "not for profit." Is the corporation being established as a profit-based business? Is the business going to be a nonprofit-based corporation? Multiple options exist within nonprofit structure and tax status, including the option to hire employees, establish as a charitable trust, etc.

Check with the state/province office of corporations to review the regulations!

One or more business attorneys should review your choice to be sure you have checked on all the local and regional regulations. They will typically provide a free appointment to review your initial business structure. The best tax status for your corporation should be reviewed with one or more accountants.

5. Necessary Permits and Licenses
The city or regional licensing office will provide the outline of the regulations required to operate your type of business within their community. Typically, you will be required to obtain a business license to operate the business in each location, whether you hire contractors and employees or not. The requirements regarding licensing and permits can often be double-checked through one of many resources: 1) Internet, 2) library, 3) city or regional clerk's office, 4) chamber or community service office for businesses in the region, 5) labor workforce or employment department offices in your area, etc., before operating your business in the community.

For the identification of your business in legal documents, as a sole-proprietor or partnership, the business ID number will be your social security or ID number. If the business becomes a for-profit or a not-for-profit corporation, the assigned taxpayer ID number will become the ID number for the business.

6. Subcontractors
Do not start by creating all contracts for subcontractors "from scratch." Obtain sample contracts to review before you prepare the draft copy to be examined by an attorney. Copies are typically available at a law library or the public library. The samples will refer to a similar business type and it is important to review the outline before you begin to establish the initial agreements or contracts for involving any independent contractors or subcontractors.

Example: I obtained a sample Practice Management Agreement for the various types of physicians who would become involved in my corporation. I worked directly with attorneys to be sure I did not break the law. Working with my attorneys, I learned that a nonlicensed physician is not able to sign a contract and split fees for services provided by a licensed physician.

Again, one or more business attorneys will be available to consult with you and review your contracts before you issue or sign the contracts.

7. Employees

An organizational development plan needs to be enacted regarding the type of business structure you are establishing. This organizational plan will help to define the types of employees you plan to hire and at what stage of your business development the positions will be required. The organizational development structure, job descriptions, and options for the plan are available within books in the public library or within the labor workforce or employment department in your area. The staff will often assist you with the process, as you will be contributing jobs to the region. Therefore, take advantage of their expertise. They are there to assist business owners, especially since your business plans match their community goals!

The various options within organizational development books in the library are extremely helpful. After reviewing a few sample organizational development structures or charts, you will be able to adapt a chart that matches your hiring goals and plans.

The structure will help you to define which employees are going to become a direct or an indirect cost:

- Direct employees are those employees involved in the immediate production process of your business.
- Indirect employees are not involved in the direct production or service phases of your business, but they are required to complete the tasks of the business.

Typically, office staff will be included in the indirect category when you are producing a product. If, however, your business is a professional service type of business, i.e., engineering or architectural, the office staff may be in the direct cost category if they are involved in the production of the service. This is an important cost to consider, so it needs to be defined during the start-up and expanding phases of the business. Therefore, we will further define this section of your plan within chapters 6 and 7.

Part-time or temporary employees are often available on a contractual basis through employment agencies. You will pay a percentage of the hourly rate to cover costs for benefits and workers' compensation insurance, but you would pay a similar rate for an employee for whom you would be obligated to pay all employment costs, and you would not be able to end the agreement at the end of the day. For a temporary employee, you are only obligated for the pay rate during the hours of the contract, which can be terminated at any time. When you no longer need the assistance, or if the costs dip into your profits, you can end the agreement with little notice. This is an advantage during the early days of a new division or the launch of a new business, since tasks are required in the initial development phase that may not continue into the next phase of the business.

Obligations of the Employer

You need to know all the laws regarding hiring employees, establishing payroll, payroll taxes, liability and other insurances, hours of work, benefits that are paid in the area where you are conducting business, etc. Spend some time with the labor, workforce, or employment development office in your area. They will have the simplified outline of the labor or workforce regulations and they will provide the required posters for your business type and industry. The Internet and library often include reference sources that can confirm this information.

8. Legal Status

Review the business's legal status with at least three attorneys and the tax status with at least three licensed CPAs. Until a business attorney and a CPA review the legal and tax section of the business structure, it is not finalized! Set appointments with top business attorneys and CPAs in your area. Compare notes before making decisions about your business structure, especially regarding which professional you will accept advice from in the future.

Each CPA and attorney will provide a perspective according to their field of expertise and how they do business. During the "free" initial appointment, check on each key point on your list, and if a question is posed in a later appointment, call the prior expert(s) and review the question. Be sure to obtain the same information from the same type of expert before reviewing the specific facts and choosing your representative.

From this day forward, your business "health" will depend

upon their advice, and you will be paying a fee for that advice. The relationship needs to be based upon good facts and trust, so take your time in making the final decision.

Congratulations!
Defining your business is the toughest part of the planning process. You've taken the first big and powerful step.

Building Your Seven Step Business Plan

1. Structure

   A. Business Type:

   B. Industry:

   C. Legal Status (Corp., LLC, etc., and either C or S, etc.):

2
Placement

Where Will Your Business Fit Within Your Industry and the Marketplace?

The biggest mistake owners make is thinking we have the most unusual business idea, it does not exist in the marketplace yet, and we are going to get our business to the consumers first. This might be true with a one-in-a-million idea. However, our chances of developing a one-in-a-million idea . . . well, since I gave away the secret, you already know the odds!

Immediately I am concerned when a client says we have to hurry and develop the business plan before someone else steals the idea. Ideas are out there. We do not have the market cornered on any idea. Very few people with ideas will proceed and develop the idea into a tangible entity, a business that will become part of the marketplace. But you are the exception to the rule.

Now that you have set out to pursue your idea, it is important that you continue to follow and recognize the needs of the market that initially inspired you. Understanding the placement of your business within the industry is as important today as it will be every day you are in business. Placement will continue to be a critical, evolving decision each month.

Too many businesses forget to stay current regarding the trends within the industry and the business market in general. The business process is a fluid process, so do not plan on making a decision regarding placement and then setting your business idea into a concrete base and forcing it to hold up to this statement for more than a few weeks. This is why I absolutely recommend reviewing the Seven Step Business Plan form each month.

This phase of planning your business is a good time to meet and interview the experts, including CPAs and attorneys, and consult many trusted friends and professionals. List the names on your notepad each time you think of a friend in business. Meet with them and share your business description and chosen tax and legal status choices. Their feedback will become extremely valuable as you progress through the process. Your trusted friends and known business professionals may provide the names of one or more businesses you will want to research.

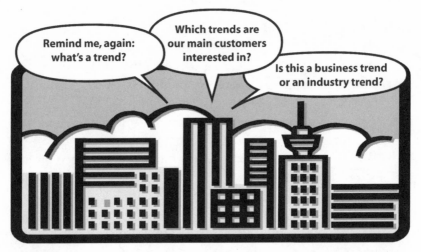

Customers

If you think everyone is your customer, take a second look at the facts about your business and what it will provide to the community. Who your customers are and what they require is critical information to know. Defining your customers will assist you in the process of matching your business with the top competitors in your industry.

Are you in business to work with the government or other businesses, or with the public? Once you know your type of customer, discern where they are located and when or how the purchase will take place. Are you in a business where it is important that you can provide the product or service, or will the customer decide based upon the price at which you can provide it?

Do customers need your products or services on a daily basis or less often? What is the level of demand for your product from each customer? Is your main customer from one gender or specifically from an age group that represents the young or old? If you are providing products or services for a specific group of customers, will they be making the purchasing decision or will someone in their life be making the decision for them?

Knowing your customers and their decision-making process is critical. Begin by defining three categories of customers since you may not be sure of the exact type of customer you will be serving. Categories might be listed as:

1. Ultimate (customers who would buy your main products or services as well as any additional, related products or services)
2. Average (customers who would buy your main products or services and consider related products or services)
3. Buyer (customers who would buy only your business's main products or services)

Top Competitors:
Learning the Industry Marketplace

You have to know your competition and how they are doing business within your industry. Begin with the title "Competitors" on a page of your notepad. Add names to your list each time you identify a business in your industry. Expand your list and add all related businesses, increasing the scope and parameter of your search. This list will also help you gain an objective view of how the various businesses affect your business and your industry.

When you think the list is complete, share it with at least three trusted friends. Their input will assist you in searching for additional facts about the businesses in your industry.

Caution: If you decide to go forward with a narrow viewpoint regarding your competition, you will hamper your business growth potential. If you use a larger database now, you will gain a more objective viewpoint about your business plans, and you will set the stage to continually be on top of what is happening in your industry and the marketplace.

If you are still having difficulty making a list of your competitors, try using hindsight to gain 20/20 vision. Make a list of the businesses that are not in a position to compete with your business. Then, remove them from your list obtained from the phone book, chamber directory, or business directory and review how the remaining businesses do business, how they list their business, and how they advertise their products and services.

Competitive Edge

To understand your competition, begin from the perspective of the consumer/customer and find out why they purchase products and services from your competitors. What are the advantages? Is the business convenient? Are the products better priced? Do they offer greater value or better service? Has the business developed a relationship due to an excellent reputation in the industry?

Review the list of strengths of each business and distinguish the real strengths of the business in the marketplace from the perceived strengths. How the businesses are perceived is based upon how they express their image through advertising and marketing campaigns. With these two business directions in mind, review each competing business on your list one more time.

Establish a Competitive Strategy

As you begin to identify competitors, summarize their business facts.

Name:

Structure (corporation, sole-proprietorship, etc.):

Annual sales (from their annual report):

Longevity in the marketplace:

What works about their business (characteristics that draw consumers/customers):

What doesn't work (characteristics that do not attract consumers/customers):

Involvement in the community (business facts available through chamber(s) of commerce, business and trade association(s), libraries, colleges/universities, and newspapers/magazines):

Additional notes based upon your observations:

The following questions will help you research what you need to know about your competition.

1. What are the names of the top businesses in your industry?

It is important to start right here with the first names

that come to mind and then keep looking until you know everything about every business within your industry.

2. What are the names of the top businesses in your community?

You will be amazed when you see how creative people are with the names of their businesses. This is good if it draws more customers. If the name of the business is not immediately recognized with your business products and services or it puts your business at the end of the list in the yellow pages or chamber directories, keep looking for more names.

a. In your surrounding area.

Begin in your local community. Check out every business that is similar or related to your business. Are any of the businesses coming together to market or promote the business?

b. In your county/region, state/province, or nation.

Once you know your community, begin looking at the business directories in your county/region, state/province, or nation. Once you have identified the businesses, look at the list again and analyze their structure and marketing techniques. How are they promoting their business? Are they promoting their businesses together with related businesses?

c. In the yellow pages, local advertising, radio, TV, and print media, etc.

You will be ahead of the game when you know all of the promotional options the related businesses are using within your industry. Since new businesses are opening every month, be sure to check the options on a regular basis.

d. On the Internet and within the Internet directory and search engines.

Whether you are going to be a business on the Internet or not, include businesses within the Internet directory and search engines on your list of businesses researched.

3. What are the tag lines and catch phrases that exist in your industry?

An easy way to think about this process is to picture a billboard about your business. What would you include on the billboard? If you think of a background to draw your customers, would it be a dynamic color? Would it include a picture?

With that background firmly in your mind, what would you say? What color and type of graphics would you use for the words? What would be your promotional phrase about your business? Phrases should be easy to remember and they should immediately catch the attention of current and future customers.

Think about the billboards that you remember. What caught your attention, the color, the picture, or the words? Do you remember the tag line? Your goal is a well-structured phrase that will draw the attention of customers to the best aspects of your business. The customers should remember the phrase for a long, long time and be glad they did!

A billboard or ad phrase being remembered is only half of the assignment.

4. What is your industry known for within the marketplace? How will your business contribute to the industry and the marketplace?

What are the key points your business identifies within the industry and the marketplace? To capture a special market niche, identify your specific business contributions to the industry. The goal is to set your business apart from each business in the industry and the marketplace.

5. What are you producing and providing for your consumers/customers?

Now that you know what the businesses in your industry are

producing and providing, list the many ways your business is unique and special in the industry and the marketplace. What will you do to capture the interest of the consumers/customers in your market area?

6. What does your business contribute to the community (local, national, global)?

Once you know what sets your business apart, list the contributions your business will be making in the community, whether your business community is your town, city, county/region, state/province, nation, or the world.

7. What are the key characteristics about your business? How can the key characteristics be defined for consumers/customers?

Now, take a moment and look over your specific ideas. Where does your passion for your business lead you? This is a significant statement about how your business is done, especially since you are in charge of how it is developed.

Image: Perception of Your Business Within the Marketplace

1. What makes your business unique in the industry?

Using your answers from the questions above, you can simply state what sets your business apart from the other businesses in your industry and in the marketplace.

2. How are your business products and services introduced to the marketplace?

At this point, you will begin to see exactly how you will introduce your products and services and what needs to be said about your business to launch your business into the marketplace.

3. What is the perception of your business in the marketplace?

Since you know how the related businesses are perceived through advertising and the length of time they have been devoted to the community and the industry, you have a more objective viewpoint regarding your business idea and how it is viewed by your consumers/customers.

4. As a spokesperson/business, what are your strengths?

What are the personal and business contributions you will add to the industry? Will your strengths result in a new revenue stream being developed that does not currently exist within the industry? The business will be an extension of you, so what do you bring to the process?

5. What can consumers/customers count on if your business is in the marketplace?

Will your business provide enhanced products or services? Will you be personalizing your services to match the needs of consumers/customers? Will specific benefits be evident because you establish your business within the industry and the marketplace?

Distinguish Your Business from Every Other Business in the Marketplace

Develop powerful words regarding how your business is unique and different in the industry and the marketplace. What makes your business distinct and different? What will attract the customers?

Building Your Seven Step Business Plan

2. Placement

A. Top Competitors:

1.
2.
3.

B. Image Within the Industry:

3
Leadership

The most important statement you can make about your business is the statement you make about yourself and your involvement within each phase of the business. The statement you make about each member of your leadership team closely follows the importance of the statement you make about yourself. The reason you are the owner of the business, the director of the division, or the leader of the team is exactly what will draw people, as investors, vendors, and/or customers, to the business.

Your leadership ability is critical, as is your ability to inspire others. The leadership skills and abilities develop into the team strengths that are going to be evident in the business structure and help sell the business to each customer, vendor, employee, and business. Remember, you are not able to be all things to all people within the business, and you are not able to be all things to all people within the team. Each leader plays

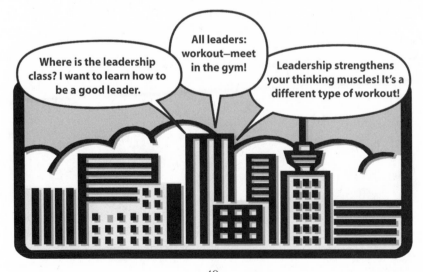

a specific role, and the team's strengths and support in areas of weakness will define the overall strengths of the business.

When you detail your involvement, be sure to align your statements with the phrases you wrote to describe your business today and your plans for the future as of this phase of the process. Then, be sure to receive feedback from a variety of people. This statement will need to remain flexible in order to complement the plans for each aspect of the business as you continue to refine them.

In this statement, your contribution to the bottom line needs to be apparent. Your understanding of the budget and cash flow as well as your financial plans to break even and expand beyond planned profit levels have to be clear to anyone reading your statement. In addition, the participation of each of the leaders on the team and within the business must be defined and included.

As you continue through the process of developing your business plan, you will be adding to your personal statement. Skills relevant to each phase of the business process need to be included in that statement. For example, when you define your marketing plan, you need to add a statement regarding how the business and community or customers benefits from your marketing perspective.

Begin outlining your personal statement by matching your expertise and plans with the following:

1. The business concept, your vision and mission, and how it will develop
2. The production or operational plan and how you affect the way it will unfold
3. The marketing and financial plan and how contingencies will be handled
4. Specific goals and methods of measuring the progress and achievements

Sometimes we amaze ourselves. In fact, when I was asked to describe my entrepreneurial interests and my mentors, I was a woman of few words—shocking, yet true. I said it was exciting for me, and I had a few mentors in different areas of my life, but I was the first one in my family to establish a business.

Within moments I found out this statement was not the truth. It was suggested that I search my family tree because leaders typically have a significant list of influential people in their lives, and the most important examples are within their inner circle, their family and friends. I trusted I would not find an entrepreneur on the list. However, I was surprised to learn that many entrepreneurs are found on both sides of my family tree, and the list of influences in prior generations is just as significant as in the current generation.

Now, it is your turn. Take a moment and look at your inner circle. Who are the entrepreneurs in your family? Who are the people who significantly influence your life and decisions? What have you observed about them over the years? What is it about them, about their character and demeanor, that inspires you? Make a few notes, list the specific details, and I trust you will be able to make a powerful statement about your leadership skills and abilities that will bring a tear to your eye or at least cause you to reflect upon some powerful moments in your life.

Then, do not become shy. Each member of your team can use your insight, examples, and feedback regarding their strengths. Remember, it is a development process and they will benefit from your input. It is human to think about what we have to work on or "get fixed" in our lives before the goals can be achieved. Take time to talk about accomplishments and overcoming obstacles versus focusing upon the obstacles, because, I guarantee, there will be obstacles in the way of accomplishing your goals and your business plans. Support from the team leaders is critical to the smooth planning, development, and expansion of the business as well as the achievement of each goal while operating the business.

Leaders Identified: Description of Leaders and Company Leadership

Business Is Founded on the Decisions of the Top Leaders of the Business
Take a moment to answer the following questions about the individuals in leadership positions in your company.

1. Who are the leaders?
2. Who is accountable for each aspect of the business?
3. Who will take on assignments and successfully accomplish them?
4. Why are they the leaders for specific tasks?
5. What would support their development?
6. When you assign a task, what will your leaders be able to accomplish?

Leaders Take on the Task, Inspire the Team, and Fulfill a Leadership Role
Make a list of those who excel in the various phases of the business process.

1. Expertise in managing tasks
2. Expertise in production and performance
3. Expertise in the overall operation
4. Expertise in serving the needs of customers
5. Expertise in promoting and selling concepts, products, and services
6. Expertise in working with people
7. Expertise with budgets, projections, and cash-flow analysis

Now prepare a list of leaders for each leadership role.

1. Management
2. Production and performance standards
3. Operations
4. Service
5. Marketing and Sales
6. Human Resources
7. Accounting and Finance

Highlights: The Unique Strengths of Each Leader

Begin with a list of the highlights in the biography, or BIO, of each leader in your business.

- Experience
- Education and/or proven track record
- Professional expertise
- Industry knowledge
- Established relationships (suppliers, vendors, customers)

With these highlights in mind, a clear and distinct BIO needs to be written for each team member.

Leaders continue to develop and grow, so each leader

should be able to add to the BIO on a regular basis. Refine and update the BIO with passion. Be sure to include accomplishments and a succinct description of achievements that have been accomplished since the previous BIO was developed. Plan on the BIO continually being a work in progress.

Expansion of the industry and community involvement of the leaders improves the bottom line of the business.

Developing a Leadership BIO

An example is provided to use as a guide while you are developing the BIO of each leader. Study the example that I have provided based on my own experience.

International Business Coach/Keynote Conference Speaker

Who, What, Where, and for Whom
Sheila Holm, international "balanced life coach," positively affects the life of each participant in businesses, seminars, and conferences around the world.

Specifics: Matching to Consumer/Customers
Ms. Holm's unique tools and techniques evoke immediate, positive, bottom-line strategies. Her marketing and operations strategies, specifically identified for each life, business, and industry, produce profitable, long-term results confirmed within reports from clients after tracking 30 to 230 percent increases in profitability based upon revelations gained during the initial meeting. During the past two decades, her coaching tools and techniques have improved the lives and businesses of thousands of conference and

seminar participants, business leaders, owners, and management teams on each continent.

Leadership Strengths

Due to her dynamic leadership style, staff members and customers immediately recognize the changes in their lives and businesses and the impact upon their family, peers, industry, and community. Participants consistently acknowledge her ability to ignite dialogue and inquiry throughout their lives and businesses. Leadership immediately emerges within each life and partnership, i.e., with each staff member, family member, customer, and vendor. This dialogue immediately expands into powerful business relationships, partnerships, and profitable strategic alliances, which have positively catapulted their lives, families, and businesses to the next level of success.

Background, Development, Contribution

Ms. Holm has lectured throughout the university system at various colleges and universities throughout the country and the world. Her lectures have included both industry and employment trends as well as her "balanced life coaching" tools and techniques. She agrees to participate in additional meetings and lectures while traveling as a keynote conference speaker and seminar leader to inspire the next generation within every community extending her an invitation.

Meeting and Exceeding Goals and Expectations

The executive business and industry coaching techniques improve each area of life, which causes the owners and the members of their management and support teams to seek "balanced life coaching." This inspired Ms. Holm to develop the practical tools for her clients within a game board format, causing clients to realize they are actually playing the game in their lives and their businesses. With this recognition, clients are able to successfully structure their game plan within moments each day.

Prior Achievements

Her unique training program caused the United States government to extend an annual federal contract to her to provide the entrepreneurial training course for the defense industry. The 100 percent success rate of the program provided automatic annual contract renewals for both the defense and aerospace industries, where major industry participants such as General Dynamics, Hughes, Northrop Grumman, and Lockheed Martin benefited.

Prior Background

Sheila also founded and operated a California corporation. She obtained degrees from top universities and directed both marketing and human resources departments for major corporations such as AVCO, TraveLodge International, SONY Corporation, and Pacific West.

Personal Interests: Defining Personal Characteristics

Sheila is actively engaged in numerous community and charitable activities. She also enjoys oil painting, volleyball, tennis, and golf, while her special interest is high-speed car rallies, especially on California mountain routes.

Write Your Own BIO

Who, What, Where, and for Whom

Define your contribution to the business development. How will your expertise benefit the consumer/customer when the business provides the product or service in the marketplace? Who will you serve? What will you manage, produce, or sell? Where will you produce, service, or sell?

Specifics: Matching to Consumers/Customers

Determine your contribution to the community and the marketplace. What are the unique aspects that set the business and your expertise apart from the competition? What can consumers/customers count on? Have other consumers/customers experienced these results? Do results vary for various consumer/customer groups?

Leadership Strengths

Clarify your contribution to the overall business: each team member, department and division, and all in the community who will benefit from the products and services of your business being provided in the marketplace. What is your contribution to the business structure within your scope of direct responsibility, and how will your additional areas of expertise enhance the business, including management, operations, production, sales and marketing, public and customer relations, and financial status of the business?

Background, Development, Contribution

Begin by matching your professional background with technical skills and abilities. Then, add development phases of the business and the planned contribution to the community, aligned with your background, skills, and abilities.

Meeting and Exceeding Goals and Expectations

Highlight areas, both personal and professional, where accomplishments have surpassed the planned goals and expectations, whether the results are based upon a single project or a long-term or major program.

Prior Achievements

Identify specific personal and business achievements accomplished during your career. Be sure to relate the achievements to the business plans and goals.

Prior Background

Prepare a succinct statement regarding the business background and directly relate it to the expertise identified within the plan.

Personal Interests: Defining Personal Characteristics

Distinguish the leadership areas you are involved in within the community and marketplace. Stress the areas where your passion is evident in hobbies, the arts, or sports and areas where you personally contribute to the community.

Building Your Seven Step Business Plan

3. Leadership

    A. Leader. Always a leader or trained to lead (BIO attached)?

    B. Strengths. Each leader BIO (attached):

4
Purpose and Highlights

Why does the business exist? Why does your business need to be established within the industry? Are you going to provide a new or revised product or better service?

Purpose Statement

The purpose statement is your billboard statement. If you were announcing your business to the community today, what would you put on the billboard? What do you want the potential consumers/customers to know about your products and services? The purpose statement must clearly and distinctly describe why your business should be in existence in the industry and the marketplace.

What Is the Basis of Your Business?

Before writing your purpose statement, think about how your business handles the following important aspects:

1. Consideration of consumer needs
2. Meeting consumer/customer expectations
3. Development and production of profit

With these characteristics in mind, fully define the purpose of your business. Your purpose should reflect how your business will address the three aspects of business listed above.

Begin by writing down a few words that set your business apart from the rest of the businesses within the industry and in your community. Then, describe why you think your business should exist in your community or why it should be introduced into a larger marketplace.

Many people respond: "I'm starting a business to make

money." That is an adequate answer, but not an answer that addresses the purpose. Clearly, the business should make money. In fact, even the IRS will not allow a business to be "written off" for more than three years since it is considered a hobby at that point.

Clarity regarding the business purpose is critical to the successful start-up and expansion of your business. For example, if I am not able to describe the benefits provided by coaching executives and their management teams to the next level, I should not expect clients to pay a fee for the services.

Next, describe your business in specific detail. In the purpose statement, give the customers a great reason to care about your business being in the community by motivating them to rush into the marketplace and buy your products/services. Refine the statement until you, as a customer, would be convinced to buy!

To support the development of the purpose statement, review the highlights of the leadership team and the business. The phrases describing the leaders and the members of their teams will become the basis of your business and it will support the powerful phrase that becomes the purpose statement.

Highlights: Unique Characteristics of the Business

Take a moment to get a glass of water or a cup of coffee, and turn the ringer off on *all* your phones and communication devices. That's right, each and every one, whether it is the buzzer to let you know you have an e-mail or the ringer on your cell or PDA, each one needs to be turned off before you begin. Find a very comfortable location, a location that will allow you to be relaxed and focused when you begin listing the highlights that set your business ideas and plans apart.

Specific Strengths within the BIO of the Leaders and Business

Prepare phrases that confirm the highlights within each BIO. As you reread them, a good way to check the content and be sure the phrases are significant is to ask yourself the questions, "Do the phrases stand out? Do they speak to me?"

Example: Our marketing director provided industry marketing research for the national survey conducted this year for our industry. Our training director is a credentialed instructor, and our seminars meet the requirements for continuing education credits to update professional licenses.

Unique Strategic Alliances You Have Developed

List each business, supplier, vendor, and community or customer group you have included within your business BIO. Then, list the unique aspects of the relationships and identify the specific ways this alliance will benefit the business.

Example: Strategic alliances with our key suppliers will eliminate all up-front production costs for materials and supplies required to develop our products.

Special Business Relationships You Have Developed within Your Marketplace

Have you established special and unique relationships with key vendors or community organizations? Are you going to barter with any of the businesses on the list to increase the cash flow of your business? Are you involved in a barter organization with printers, suppliers, etc.?

Example: Contracts with a local printer include all printing costs for marketing, advertising, and promotional materials. Contracts were obtained from three major corporations due to our donations for a local community fundraiser.

Contributions Your Business Is Making within and for the Community

List the organizations in the community that will benefit from the contributions, donations, or participation of your business during its developmental phase. Then, add your plans for further expansion and development in the community. These organizations will enhance and assist with the recognition of your business in the community and the marketplace, so keep this list as a work in progress and solicit the assistance of foundations in the community.

Example: Contracts are established with twenty-five non-profits to provide certificates for their monthly events, which supplies income up front to cover all labor costs for the business.

Having completed your list of contributions your own business is making to the community, review the list you made in chapter 2 of community contributions from your competitors. Do not limit the list to the organizations, youth groups, or activities they are involved with at this time. It will benefit your business to be in the forefront of a special cause and become known as a business that gives back to a community that supports your business plans, growth, and expansion.

Then, take a break and call or e-mail a couple of trusted friends. Ask them to review the list and add names of organizations.

Business Statement

Now you are ready to define the key facts about the business. Your business statement should provide basic contact and operating information.

Begin simply. Who is the owner? Who are the owners/partners, general or limited?

What is the name of the business? Have you considered a potential logo? Will the name lend itself to a dynamic logo that customers will easily recognize? Where will the business name appear in the phone book and within which category? Is the business name a name that will draw customers?

As soon as you have selected the perfect name for your business, you need to file a "doing business as," or DBA, notice with your regional recorder's office. The DBA filing should confirm your research that the name is not being used by any other business in your region.

Owner(s) —————————————— *Business* ——————————————

After establishing your business name, identify the address. The address of each business owner/partner will match the address of his or her personal financial statement.

The business location is an extremely important decision. Will customers walk into your business location or will you be providing the products/services at a location in the marketplace or through a distribution source? The business address should be the right location for the customers to be able to easily reach you in order to purchase your products/services. Your choice should clearly align with your business plan at this stage of your business. However, it may change as your business expands and as your business structure changes.

Once you have chosen the location, you need to decide if the mail should be delivered to a post office box address or to the business's physical address. The address will become part of your business DBA and license filings.

Owner Address ————————————— *Business Address* —————————————

City ————————— *State* ——— *Zip* ———   *City* ————————— *State* ——— *Zip* ———

Business License: Typically, the regulation for the business is to license the business in the city and/or region where you will be conducting the business. If you are going to hire an employee, the business license is required before you complete the hiring process.

If you operate as a sole-proprietor or partnership, the business ID number will be your ID/social security number. If the business becomes a corporation, for profit or not for profit, the taxpayer ID number will become the ID number for the business. The ID number will appear on the license.

Staff License: Be sure to include all professional license information for each staff member.

> If it's a sole-proprietor business, do I have a job?

> Yes. You're a great employee. Sole-proprietor means I'm the only owner, but I'm not able to do everything alone.

Business Permits: List all permits obtained to do business in the location you have selected. This will confirm to the investors, partners, and financial institutions that your business is being developed on a solid base because you have researched the facts and reviewed the regulations before opening the doors.

License ——————————— *Permit* ————————————————

Your life will change the moment the business begins. Personally, I chose to obtain a voice-mail pager as a "forever" number for the business so that I can receive messages from any location around the globe. When you decide on a personal and business number to include within your plan, be sure it is a number that can be reached from any customer location at any time the business is open or available to customers.

Phone ——————————— *Phone* ————————————————

The fax number is optional. If you are going to accept fax orders for your business, it will become a critical number to include. Since fax solicitations are becoming a serious issue, you may choose to state only that it is available, rather than listing a number.

Fax ——————————— *Fax* ————————————————

Cell phone access is also optional.

Cell ——————————— *Cell* ————————————————

An e-mail address should be established for your business contacts whether it links to a business Web site or not. A Web site does add credibility to your business launch, so consider establishing a Web presence even if the site is only one page with an e-mail link or a business phone number.

E-mail ——————————— *Web site* ————————————————

Insurance is very important to the investors and financial institutions. Securing the insurance policies in advance confirms that the investment in your business will be more secure for the investors and financial institutions.

Each owner, key leader, and manager needs to be insured. The confirmation of policies in place will put everyone's mind at ease. Because in business, as in life, anything can happen, key business personnel need to be insured.

Personal and business liability insurance: Have you obtained health, disability, including long-term disability, and life insurance policies? Have you secured a business liability policy?

Assets policies: Have you obtained a policy for your personal assets? Have you obtained a policy to cover business assets and equipment in case of loss?

Insurance _____   *Insurance* _____

Building Your Seven Step Business Plan

4. Purpose and Highlights

   A. Purpose Statement:

   B. Highlights:

   C. Business Statement:

Owner(s)_____	Business_____
Address_____	Address_____
City_____ State _ Zip__	City_____ State _ Zip__
License _____	Permit _____
Phone_____	Phone_____
Fax _____	Fax_____
Cell_____	Cell_____
E-mail_____	Web site_____
Insurance_____	Insurance_____

5
Vision and Mission Statements

Plan to Succeed: Know Your Destination and Route Before Launching the Business!
The ultimate destination of your business and its journey into the future of your industry arise from a clear vision and confirmed mission statement. However, defining your vision and mission statement is not an easy process the first time. In fact, the experience is absolutely a brain-stretching process that can seem overwhelming since your business idea, like your business, is continually in development.

> *"If you do not know where you are going, any road will get you there."*

The vision allows you to see the future and potential of your business. The commitment and plan to reach the vision is defined in the mission statement. Therefore, it helps to think of the vision as the destination of your business's journey and the mission statement as the series of steps the business will take to meet the needs of the customers and fulfill upon the vision.

Every Business Idea Changes When the Vision and Mission Statements Are Defined
When I ask the new owners of a business, "What is the vision for the business?", their typical response is "To make money, of course. Work harder and sell more than anyone else." This is not the key to success. Taking off full speed ahead with a new business idea before the vision and mission

statement are clearly defined is the main reason why a start-up business will fail within the first year of business.

Defining your vision and mission statement actually replaces the working harder theory. Your vision and mission statement will become the *anchor* as your business progresses and expands. As your business adds new divisions and products, they will become the *key* to profitability and success, since this planning phase will confirm that your team is working smarter based upon a thorough, solid vision of the planned destination for the business and a planned road map to success.

Failing to plan results in a business planning to fail.

Caution: When the vision is not well defined, you will find yourself in a losing cycle:

1. Expending energy and money based upon thinking the business idea is a good idea and worth everything you can give to it
2. Working harder and harder, all the while trusting sweat equity will make the business profitable

Set Clear Vision and Mission Statements Aligned with Goals Before Money Is Involved!

Establishing your effective vision and mission statements prior to venturing into a new business or adding a new product or service to the current business will significantly increase your rate of success with the business. Focusing upon the concept being so unique that it will make money on the merits of the concept alone, especially as soon as financial investments are provided by capital venture sources to support the business growth plan, is a recipe for failure. However, when your business idea is clearly defined by your vision statement, the business idea is automatically focused on the future success of the business, confirming its viability in the marketplace. Your vision statement is actually a "reality check" for the business idea, since your vision statement confirms that your business idea has a solid chance of becoming profitable.

Vision Statement: Determining the Destination

The only source that can define the business vision for the future is you and each of the team members involved with you in the start-up or expansion phases of the business. It is important to remain clear about the vision for the future of your business. It will catapult the business forward, far beyond your initial start-up or expansion plans to pay for the overhead expenses.

Your vision needs to be your vision,
clearly stated, to be successful!

The Business Vision Statement

Clearly state your vision of the business in one brief sentence. Every potential customer needs to be able to immediately understand what your business is planning to do and what your business will accomplish within the community based upon your vision statement. Errors in planning are immediately recognized by customers, so it is important to check the accuracy of your vision statement before proceeding.

Your vision statement should possess the following four characteristics:

1. Defines the marketplace being served by services or products
2. Identifies the destination of the business
3. Aligns your goals with the future plans of the business
4. Answers the questions:
   a. Who is served by your services/products?
   b. Where is this business headed?
   c. When will the business arrive at and surpass break-even profit levels?

Consider the last three questions while picturing your future business path as a train heading toward its destination. Who are the passengers served by your method of transportation? Where is the train (your business) headed? Chicago? Perhaps Hong Kong? Yes, I realize you need to change the mode of transportation to actually travel to Chicago, and especially for Hong Kong, and I am grateful you recognize this need. This is why the review of the business "in the future" is so critical. The business will require changes in the mode of operating and marketing, depending on its ultimate destination. Too, the financial structure will need to be modified as the business continues to develop so that it can reach its goal, or profit.

Business Community and Marketplace

Your vision statement needs to be specific regarding all the customers who will benefit from your products or services. Regulations and requirements for specialized products or services within each region need to be considered and fully defined by you before you prepare your vision statement. Your products or services may meet the needs of customers within:

1. One town or region of a state or province
2. An entire state or province
3. One country
4. The global marketplace

A business plan lacks credibility if your vision statement lacks evidence of research, knowledge, and understanding of the regulations and laws required to market specialized products or services in the region as described. Planning for a local business in one town or region is very different from planning for a business that extends throughout a nation or the international community. Regulations and laws for many products and services vary by town, region, state or province, and nation.

Should Your Business Proceed as Planned?

Typically, more than 85 percent of business ideas suggested as a developing business plan do not proceed as *originally* planned. Reviewing your business idea in the form of your vision statement and visualizing how the business will progress is critical to determining if your goals are actually aligned with the business development plan.

Business Concept Aligned to Business Vision and Goals

Often at the beginning of a movie, the theatre provides some trivia information. One of the best trivia questions on the list is the question showing three options for the original title of the movie versus the title we recognize as the one marketed in the theatres. The titles often appear unmarketable compared to the movie title we recognize. The difference between the original movie title and the actual movie title is significant. The actual title is realized during the development process, when the vision of the movie comes into focus for the staff working in production each day. It is the same process for a business vision: a business concept is developed and molded into shape over time as more and more facts are realized.

To make the process a little less painful while preparing your vision statement, I trust a few examples of adjustments to the initial vision and goals will be beneficial to compare the process with the development of your business idea.

Test the Idea

Business ideas can appear to be good enough for you to pursue until it makes a profit. But you do not have to be out of pocket financially before you are able to test the idea to be sure it will be profitable. Client examples are being provided within this chapter to confirm the fact that the vision and mission statements are the litmus test for your business idea.

Client Example 1
Business: T-shirts with a unique design
Goal: Become profitable within three months
Initial Vision: T-shirt sales to pay costs and a new car
  payment

Problem with the Vision
The vision is limited and not aligned with short-term goals, let alone future goals. Sales need to exceed overhead costs by far more than the cost of the payment for a new car. The owner needs to consider all additional costs, including the increase in insurance premiums and registration. Costs that are not considered are not included, and the business plan will

then fall short of meeting the financial needs of the business.

It is important to match the vision with the goals. The volume of T-shirts being packed and the number of boxes to be shipped from the business location defined will not meet the goals within three months.

By reviewing the facts and regulations in her community, the new owner realized the volume of T-shirts could not be shipped from a personal residence. To meet the goals, a different business location was required. The change in business location within three months increased the monthly budget. Therefore, the decision to add the expense of a new car needs to be reconsidered.

Adjustment of the Business

The owner arranges to sell her product through television and Internet sales organizations. She also establishes the business in a retail location so that in addition to having easy access for shipping products on a daily basis, retail sales are an option. Finally, she adjusts her designs in order to sell additional products to the same customer base.

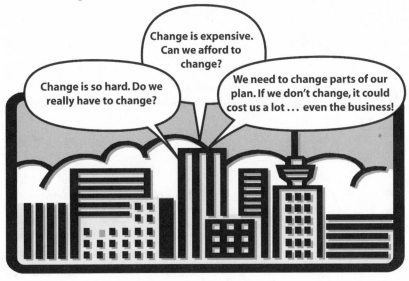

Realignment of the Vision Statement to the Purpose and Goals
Considering her cost saving options, which are as critical
as profit plans, the owner decided to live in a loft above the
retail space. She purchased a new vehicle for the delivery
of T-shirts and products to various retail locations within a
fifty-mile radius. A new car was selected. The price for the
car and all additional costs were added to the budget when
the first Internet sales program provided a solid customer
base to cover the expenses.

Client Example 2
Business: Trophies
Goal: Provide for college education of two sons, currently
    enrolled in high school
Initial Vision: Distribute trophies from business while
    operating the business in the garage

Problem with the Vision
The vision is limited and was not properly matched to the
goals. The vision includes all products sold until the date
college tuition needs to be paid for each son, but the volume of trophies being distributed to the customers from the
defined business location was not properly planned to meet
the goal. In fact, the owner was only considering two facts:

1. Trophies can be assembled and engraved by a machine
   in the garage.
2. The family will help to sell enough trophies to meet
   the goal.

Basic aspects of running the business were not planned.
The residential phone line was used to take the orders,
tying up the family phone. In addition, the phone line does
not extend to the garage. The business took off so quickly,
a centralized order area was not designated. Order forms

were in each room in the house as well as in the garage. Too, the owner did not establish a policy to receive a deposit with the order to cover inventory and shipping or delivery costs. The owner also miscalculated the budget for business cash flow to cover costs between the order and payment dates. As a result, personal finances were immediately depleted to cover inventory costs.

Adjustment of the Business

The two sons started a certificate division of the trophy business. They used their personal computers to fill the orders for the schools in their community.

They saved their income to obtain a new computer for the business and secondly to build funds for negotiating a business location outside the family home. While they were putting funds aside, they researched local retail locations available for rent. Their efforts and passion for the business paid off when they obtained a six-month rent-free retail location.

The sons surprised their parents with the new business location. The family agreed to move the entire trophy and certificate business to the retail location and they now have full use of their home and garage.

A new vision statement needs to be prepared to align with the new goals of the business.

Realignment of the Vision Statement to the Purpose and Goals

A new family business has been established that provides both certificates and trophies. Income from the trophy division of the business is deposited into the college fund account. The income from the certificate division is deposited into the business account to pay the expenses. The additional profit from the business is divided and deposited into an account for family vacations, business improvements, and future family plans. The family is also paying an extra equity payment monthly, intending to pay off the mortgage within sixty months.

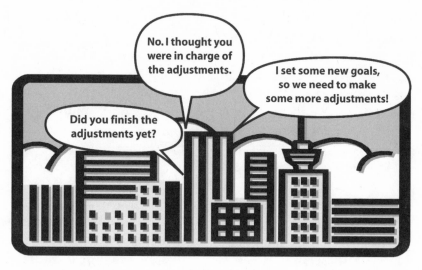

Client Example 3
Business: Recreational vehicle parts sales and distribution
Goal: Pay for recreational vehicles and vacations
Initial Vision: Provide parts seven days a week, at a discount

Problem with the Vision
The initial vision was a limited, short-term resolution. It seemed like a good idea because it was developed based upon a customer need. The owner was on a weekend trip. The boat motor failed. Parts stores were not open. When the parts were located, the prices were extremely high and the delay cost him three days of his trip.

However, the reality of the business—providing parts when they are needed and in the locations where they are needed—requires an extensive inventory, a full-time, around-the-clock call center, and a delivery system to various locations on an emergency basis.

Adjustment of the Business
Reigning in the costs of such a huge inventory was critical, so my recommendation was to specialize in parts for

speedboats only. In addition, I suggested forming strategic alliances with the manufacturers and distributors of the parts to eliminate extensive inventory and gain a support team to respond to the requests.

A new vision statement needs to be prepared to align with the new goals of the business.

Realignment of the Vision Statement to the Purpose and Goals

Agreements were established with the manufacturers and distributors to provide the inventory and cover all business and call center costs for the southern California region. The owner established a new company, receiving a bonus from the manufacturing and distribution companies upon opening the office. He promoted the services among speedboat enthusiasts, which is where he wanted to spend the majority of his time.

Sometimes a hobby can pay for itself! Sales prices were set to include a residual amount to be paid directly to his division. Therefore, he was able to pay for family expenses plus vacations and trips with the profit from the business since the manufacturer and distributor covered his operating expenses and all expenses related to the speedboat competitions and travel.

New Vision Statement

As you can see from these simple examples, adapting the business activities to the marketplace results in a new vision for all three businesses, and with the new vision they achieve even greater success. Leadership requires considering the various problems start-up businesses experience during early development. It is typical for the business vision to change, to either include or exclude specific plans from the initial business plan. As in the examples, additional products may be provided to the same customer base, or the methods for order taking, payment, or delivery of services and products may change to meet local regulations or to enhance cost and time efficiency.

A Key to Your Success

Review your vision statement not only on a regular basis, at least once a month, but also whenever ideas for new products or services, locations, or customer needs and markets change. These facts will continue to drive your business toward and beyond those goals and plans established for your business.

Your business, new division, or product line is ready for a successful launch when the following requirements are met.

1. Your vision exceeds the goal.

Research and planning is extremely important for each step. All contingency costs, especially a business location for business expansion, need to be considered and included within your plan. All additional costs need to be included and your goals redefined before your vision statement is restated to match your plans and goals for the business.

2. Your vision clearly describes your plans for the business.

Hindsight can provide 20/20 vision. Leaders must develop or hire people with near- and farsightedness so that they can envision what your business can become now and ten years from now in order to clearly see your current business and how it will develop from a future perspective. This is extremely important since human nature causes us to limit what can be produced to that within our immediate plans.

Once your vision is clear for ten years from this date, your vision can be defined for seven years, then five years, three years, and one year before the list of tasks that need to be completed within this year is prepared. Using *hindsight* from a future perspective makes it easier to see what needs to be accomplished in the next few weeks, months, and years. Then, we can begin to see how to align current goals and plans with your future goals and plans and identify the action steps required for developing your business within the first few weeks and then the next few months, before cementing plans for the year. This progressive planning allows the business plan to be based on known facts.

Realign Your Vision Statement with Your Business Purpose and Goals

Before preparing your mission statement, it is important to look at your vision statement *one more time* to be sure your purpose and vision are aligned and your business plans are still on track with your goals for the business. Once these three are fully aligned, then, and only then, is it okay to proceed with the preparation of your mission statement.

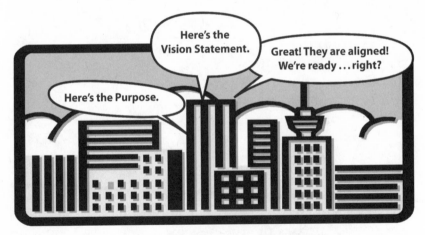

Mission Statement: Providing the Road Map

Your mission statement needs to be clear, stated frequently, and aligned to the future goals and plans before the business ever opens or expands. In addition, it must be aligned with the financial goals so the business income will exceed the expenses. The mission statement is the step-by-step description of the business commitment to provide the goods and services to the community and customers while the business proceeds toward the future goals, the planned destination. It explains how the business will reach the destination defined in the vision statement, so many tasks are defined within the statement.

The mission statement confirms that the business will:

1. Know the needs of the customers
2. Meet the needs and expectations of the customers
3. Remain current and flexible to meet the needs of the customers
4. Provide products/services that meet the needs of the customers
5. Provide products/services that remove obstacles for customers
6. Provide "superior knowledge" of the product/service
7. Confirm that the product/service sets business apart from other businesses
8. Commit to providing the products and services on a regular basis
9. Communicate the advantages of the products/services
10. Confirm how customers can better utilize products/services

Begin by listing a dozen commitments to the customers and to the community. Your list can be edited to become a succinct list of tasks the business is committed to doing or providing within the marketplace and what the customers can count on from the business.

Example: A regional bank with only one branch located in the local town is defining a few tasks within its mission statement. The bank is committed to following state/province banking regulations as well as town regulations. However, it has also drafted the following commitments:

To provide superb customer service

To provide financing options for all income levels of our customers

To commit to our customers by being open six days per week

To meet the financial needs of all citizens living in this town

To meet the financial needs of all businesses located in this town

To exceed expectations of all customers

Clarifying Your Business Niche

The vision and mission statement confirm your extensive research is complete regarding "how it is around here" for your business. It will take into account the unique and specific needs of your community and marketplace and how your business fulfills their needs.

The elements of the business plan that we have discussed through the last four chapters should be incorporated into your mission statement based on what they will enable the business to accomplish, so remember to consider those issues as you lay out your road map.

1. Structure

Business type, industry, and legal status are clearly defined.

2. Placement

Top competitors are known and their business development structure reviewed before the image of your business in the community and the marketplace is defined.

3. Leadership

Background details and strengths of the leaders are known and integrated.

4. Highlights and Purpose

Business highlights and purpose for the business to exist are defined.

Clear Vision and Mission Statement to Specifically Build and Expand the Business

If you have followed the steps outlined above and in the previous chapters, you should now have a great deal of knowledge about your business.

1. You know the type and capability of this business and the team.
2. You know the customer, the community, and their needs.
3. You know how to proceed with a successful plan in the marketplace.
4. You know why you are the business of choice for your customers.
5. You know the future destination/location of the business.
6. You have confirmed you are absolutely headed toward the destination.
7. You know the journey is aligned with the goals.
8. You know the goals are reasonable to accomplish.
9. You know the time frame you have established for the business.
10. You know your business can handle planned growth and development.

Your Sound Bite, or 15-second "Elevator or Handshake Speech"

Think of your vision and mission statements as a short person-to-person commercial or sound bite statement prepared to easily describe the business to the customer. Now you know the plans for the business are based upon solid information, so the sound bite can be prepared and become part of your personal Seven Step Business Plan.

The best description of the business is the summary of the purpose, vision, and mission statements within a 15-second sound bite, a commercial that is delivered person to person,

so anyone you meet can hear and realize why you are the leader of your team, division, or business when you describe it as you shake their hand or share an elevator. This commercial should be two succinct statements—one about you and one about the business—delivered in just 15 seconds.

Preparing Your Sound Bite

1. The final statement will require about 1.5 hours of your time to prepare.
2. The statement should not exceed 15 seconds.

A 15-second statement does not sound like a very long time to describe your expertise or your business. However, it is important to be very brief since you only have a short period to hold the focus of a potential customer. The amount of time between floors on an elevator is about 15 seconds, just enough time for an "elevator speech."

Though a typical TV commercial is 30 seconds long, it is able to use background music and visual affects. Since your business statement will not have the extra music and visuals to hold the attention of a potential customer, limit your words to a powerful 15-second message about your business.

Your speech should answer the Who, What, When, Where, Why, and How about the business and about the customers. An easy way to begin the process is to start with three columns. Write a few phrases to describe the business and the customers. Each line may not have a phrase for both the business and the customer.

	Business	**Customers**
Who		
What		
When		
Where		
Why		
How		

From this chart, the commercial sound bite should include:

1. The most powerful phrases from both lists
2. Only the descriptive words that confirm the customer advantages and benefits
3. Confirmation of the key fact that sets the business apart from other businesses

Example: International Business Coach
Clients track and report at least a 30 percent increase in their bottom line due to profitable ideas realized during our first hours of working together.

Revising Your Sound Bite

You should now have a draft statement describing your business. In the next few steps, I'll help you refine your statement to make the most of your best qualities and areas of expertise, and those of the business.

Revise your preliminary 15-second sound bite as a 30-second commercial about your business as well as your contributions and expertise. Your goal is to create a 15-second statement about your own contribution to and alignment with the business and a second 15-second statement that expresses the highlights of the business, especially the contributions to the customers and community.

Writing a commercial sounds simple, but it is not a simple process. When you view a commercial on TV, it is easy to be drawn in by a dramatic or provocative concept. After you view a commercial, you are often unaware of the product being sold. This is a problem since the most important aspect of the commercial is communicating to the customers what they need to know about your business and how they can buy your products and services. From your commercial, customers should be able to answer the following key questions:

1. Do you know the name of the business?
2. Do you know the product they are selling?
3. Are you prompted to buy?
4. Will you remember the facts after the commercial ends?

Once you have prepared the draft, prepare and refine the phrases until you have accomplished a tight 30-second commercial. Then, using the best phrases and words from each of the two parts of your commercial, see if you can reduce the 30-second commercial into a succinct 15-second business statement so it can become the "elevator/handshake" statement about you and your business, answering the Who, What, When, Where, Why, and How for your business within the industry and the Who, What, When, Where, Why, and How for your customers. Describe your business as it is positioned within the industry, especially identifying the benefits of your business within the industry and the benefits of your business for the customer.

Within the sound bite, the business purpose and vision and mission statements take shape as the personal commitment to the business and community is agreed upon, and the commitment is clear within the brief commercial statement.

Example: International Business Coaching

Purpose: Coach business owner(s) and management team(s) to the next level

Vision: Coaching international leaders to fulfill upon their plans and dreams

Mission:

To clearly hear requests of the business owner(s) and team member(s)

To provide clear direction to the team while responding to each request

To remove the mystery and provide clarity, tools, and techniques for success

To review operational, financial, and marketing plans before first session

To assist with development of a powerful vision and mission statement

To assist with the definition of operational, marketing, financial, and profitability plans, if they are not available

To provide accurate feedback and adjustments for operational, marketing, financial, and profitability plans available

To align business plan with ever-changing industry and marketing trends

To provide operational and marketing strategies to set the business apart

To provide financial and profitability strategies that support future growth

To coach the business to operate in integrity in all business transactions

To increase bottom line profitability based upon first working session

You should now be able to prepare:

1. Your vision for your current and future business
2. Your mission statement for the business within the community and the industry

3. Your commercial sound bite for the business

Building Your Seven Step Business Plan

5. Vision and Mission Statements

    A. Vision Statement:

    B. Mission Statement:

1.	2.
3.	4.
5.	6.
7.	8.
9.	10.
11.	12.

Sound Bite (15 seconds):

6
Operational and Marketing Plans

At least 90 percent of the businesses requesting coaching assistance are unable to provide an operational, marketing, or financial plan. When you write out the description of how the business will proceed according to your personal dreams and goals, you will be a step ahead of most of the businesses already in existence. So, as soon as you have a draft, an "in progress" version, celebrate, since this step places your plan and your business ahead of the curve!

Operational Plan

Planning to Production to Provision

The operational plan puts in place a specific method for how the business will proceed and accomplish the goals outlined in the vision and mission statements. At this point, the business development steps need to be outlined to support the product/service development phase from idea to selling in the marketplace.

Describe the planning of your business products and services: how and when the production of each of the products and services will take place and how they will be provided to the consumers in your community. List the steps your products or services will take to get to the customer's hands.

Steps of an Operational Plan

Step 1	Step 2	Step 3	Step 4
Production	Distribution	Customer	Payment Received
or			
Order/ Payment	Production	Distribution	Customer

or

Production	Distribution	Sold Retail	Wholesale
			Payment

Use this list of options to be sure the plan matches your dreams and goals. Remember, the business operates "according to you," so make sure the operational plan includes each of your choices and business decisions. Be sure the production process is well defined, and the expenses, labor, equipment, and capital requirements are included within your operational plan. You want to ensure anyone reviewing the plan that you have considered all variables regarding your business and industry.

Operational Structure

As you progress through the development phases, from idea to distribution, what are the main issues you will be dealing with and how will you resolve any concerns? The operational plan includes stages of development of the business. The current business status may only reflect the operational plan for a certain number of weeks or months. Then, the plan may change slightly or significantly to include expansion and growth plans. The plan confirms you are thinking through the process and considering contingencies.

Which departments will be required? Consider the timing at which each of the departments will be added during the phases of development. Include the organizational structure in your operational plan: direct and indirect labor description and costs. Perhaps you only need to employ people involved in producing the initial products, so the labor costs are all direct. However, as soon as you add administrative staff, you will be adding indirect costs to the overall business expense.

Have you obtained the required permits and licenses? Have you copyrighted, patented, or trademarked the business title, logo, or plans?

Is your business technical? Are the employees required to have specific training before being employed by your business?

Do you have to plan to train all employees to a point where they can produce/provide your products/services? Will you have to estimate the training dollars for a training schedule between the date of hire and the date when an employee can meet the production or sales quotas?

Be sure to identify the people/tasks you will be adding as the business develops and exactly what is required to meet the production/service standards so you will be fully staffed to meet the sales quotas.

This is why the operational plan is so critical. It confirms how you visualize the business plan from initial concept through the development and expansion of the business over time.

Marketing Plan

The operational and marketing plans should be fully aligned. Marketing, to support the production schedule of your business, should plan the introduction of each product/service into the marketplace. Even if your products and services are the best in the marketplace, they will not be able to market and sell themselves. You must develop a marketing plan and strategy that will launch your products and services into the marketplace.

Launching Your Products and Services

The marketing plan includes the promotional material and your marketing and sales schedule, aligned with the operational plan to support all products and services being provided to the customers.

What are the marketing trends for your business in your community, the industry, and the marketplace? A succinct description of your customer is the perfect place to begin. You will want to include a specific statement about your customer, their needs, and how you will be meeting their needs. If you are having difficulty defining the perfect customer, it may help by describing who would not be a customer, by location, etc.

What is the most significant aspect about your business? Customers can count on your business for accuracy, efficiency, and excellent service. Then, describe how you are going to expand your business and take over a larger market share within the industry and the marketplace, in the region or around the globe.

Often owners insist they want to hire marketing people because they are not interested in marketing their business themselves. Become interested. Become your best salesperson. When you become the best salesperson for the business, it immediately becomes evident to each employee, vendor, supplier, and customer.

Sales

Often, business owners forget to include the specifics regarding the sales process and how it will unfold. It is very important for you to identify your sales process and include it within your marketing plan. Will you proceed with direct sales? Will you begin with "in house" sales staff? Will you decide to contract sales with and through other businesses?

The sales process is distinct and separate from marketing, but it is related to the marketing process and part of the marketing plan. Have you researched sales of your products/services in all markets? You will want to know about the ads, the business names, the unique business characteristics that draw customers, and the pricing plans of your competitors.

Too often, I meet with a business that is isolated from their competitors. They have no idea that selling four items at $12 will not influence the customer if the competitors are selling three items at $9. Reducing the sales price to the same level is not being competitive if competitors will sell higher quotas by allowing fewer items to be purchased at the same price. This pricing example is included to make you aware how important it is to know the pricing plan of competitors. Vendor and supplier pricing opportunities should be considered before sales dates and pricing plans are finalized. Vendor options should become part of your pricing strategy.

Related Sales

Seek out each opportunity to sell a related product/service to the same customer. The cost to obtain a customer will reduce significantly if you can sell more products to the same customer.

Promoting the Business: Advertising and Public Relations

A promotional campaign publicizes products and services through advertising and public relations campaigns. If you do not have a public relations firm supporting your launch or development phases, review sample press releases and prepare a release for each business announcement. Will you be submitting ads in local, regional, or national newspapers, magazines, or phone books or through radio or TV commercials? Have you prepared a budget for the advertising campaign?

Promotional programs can be launched through other businesses. Often, a card or coupon can be distributed by related businesses or you can participate in advertising campaigns with related or community businesses and share the costs. Consider all options and costs before setting prices and establishing sales dates.

Contributing or donating a product or service through a local event can provide extensive promotional and public relations coverage for your business. The event sponsors and participants will recognize your business and the announcements and promotional materials will provide advertising for your business.

It is critical to evaluate the marketing budget options before making your final decisions.

Marketing and Operational Plans Supported by Strategic Alliances

Marketing also benefits from the successful establishment of strategic alliances. Marketing and operational plans, and teams, need to align from A to Z regarding how products and services will be created, developed, and provided to the customers. Pricing of the product/service will be based upon the choices of how the business will operate and it will be enhanced by the strategic alliances established.

> *Strategic alliances are critical to the development of a profitable business.*

Forming strategic alliances is a critical step in the initial phase of your business. Establishing these alliances with your vendors, suppliers, service providers, and customers in the business planning stage can often replace investors or start-up funding for your new business, division, or product line.

Many businesses accept payments and ship in six to eight weeks. Therefore, the cash is in the bank before they purchase the supplies and produce the product. To protect themselves from the "return" fee, they often add the base costs within the shipping figure. This is why the shipping costs are typically high. This decision is significant not only for your business stability, especially in the early stages, but also for your continued success and profitability.

Strategic alliances ease the monthly overhead stress level and drastically reduce the overhead expenses since the agreements are typically established to supply the main business supplies, services, and ongoing needs without cash. Again, this is also why products are often ordered or purchased with delivery promised to customers in six to eight weeks. With this business strategy, the business is able to collect the full retail payment and shipping and handling funds in advance of providing the products or services to the customers. All production costs, payments to vendors, and distribution sources can be paid before delivery of the product or services.

Types of Strategic Alliances

Strategic alliances vary, but each type benefits your business operation:

1. For examples suppliers or vendors can provide required supplies and services so you can proceed with your business without paying at the time of purchase, allowing a delay in the date of payment until you receive

payment from customers for your products or services. For example a clothing designer needs fabric and supplies to proceed with the designs for the next season, so her suppliers allow her to begin payment for the material upon the designated sales date of the designs rather than upon delivery of the supplies.

2. Related businesses, especially businesses within the other phases of the business process, can provide required products and/or services without advance payment in return for your patronage. When you fulfill upon your own phase of the business and receive payment from

your customers, you are able to pay the amount owed to strategic alliance business. For example, a business in your industry specializing in the distribution phase does not require payment for delivering products to your customer until you receive the payment.

3. Customers can serve as a strategic alliance when your business requests and receives deposits or prepayments before the products or services are prepared or delivered. Therefore, the expenses within the monthly budget, the overhead, and the vendors can be paid on a timely basis.

Marketing Strategy

A good marketing strategy requires an understanding of all aspects of the business process and the plans previously set in place for other phases of the business.

The Five Key Plans Utilized in a Marketing Strategy

Plan	Purpose
Advertising	publicity through radio, TV, print media, billboards
Public Relations	press releases to inform community of business developments
Marketing	apprise consumers of all available products/services
Promotional	launch the business into the market

| Sales | place, raising consumer awareness promote qualities of in-house or contracted sales staff |

30-Second Commercial for Your Business

When you are sold on your business idea, and you can clarify the idea and the benefits within a 30-second statement that convinces you, then the vendors, other businesses, and customers will be sold on your business as well.

It will be simple to create the 30-second statement about your business, right? Wrong! Even though you have prepared a draft and now you have researched and collected stacks of facts about your business, you have changed your business, whether slightly or significantly, since you prepared a statement a few pages/moments ago.

Remember, a good estimate is that it will take about one hour of your effort to create 10 seconds of the concise, succinct commercial statement about your business.

To begin the process, it will help to fill in the phrases that come to mind about your business type, industry, and customers. The statement should answer the Who, What, When, Where, Why, and How about the business, industry, and customers. This is not about what you can provide; it is all about what the customers can expect from your business. An easy way to begin the process is to start with the following columns:

	Business	Type	Industry	Customers
Who				
What				
When				
Where				
Why				
How				

Set aside a few moments to write a few powerful phrases

about your unique aspects of the business, products, and services. Add to the list of phrases each time you hear a commercial and like the wording or the intention of the statement. Use words that describe the business and the customers. Each line should include a powerful phrase for both the business and the customer.

Then, work with the phrases and adjust them until they form a powerful statement about your business. Keep refining each phrase until you are so excited about the products and services, you have to go out and buy them—now!

The commercial should define your business and include:

1. The most powerful phrases from business type, industry, and customer lists
2. Only the descriptive words that confirm customer advantages/benefits
3. Confirmation of key facts that set your business apart from other businesses
4. The reason(s) the customer should choose your business products/services

With the wisdom you have gained through this process, test the idea!

Make Sure Your Commercial Serves Your Purpose

For months, a well-known company ran an ad on TV stations around the globe. People were repeating the simple phrase and humming the music, but they were unable to identify a product or company involved with the ad. The ad drew the attention of newscasters and talk-show hosts on each continent, but consumers were surveyed and even though they could quote the ad, they had no idea which company was running it. This is not a good result after spending marketing budget dollars to repeat the TV commercial until it received global recognition.

The concept was an attention grabber, but if the business name or product/service is not the focus of the attention, the commercial does not serve the purpose. Be sure you are setting your business apart from the rest and promoting your business, products and/or services within your commercial!

Building Your Seven Step Business Plan

6. Operational and Marketing Plans

   A. Operational Plan:

   B. Marketing Plan:

7
Financial and Profit Plans

Prepare a thorough personal and business financial statement. Then, prepare a proposed budget and use the wisdom gained through preparing the financial statements and budget to prepare the cash flow and profit plans.

Where do you begin? The first document you need to prepare is your personal financial statement. It is important for anyone reviewing your documents to know how you handle your debts and invest your money. This information is a clear indicator to investors, strategic alliances, financial institutions, and limited liability company participants how you will handle the money invested in the business. How you state your personal financial status is critical to the formation of the financial section of your business plan.

Return on Investment

After weeks of studying sample financial forms, meeting with accountants, and drawing upon every ounce of

accounting knowledge I could remember from college, I trusted I was ready. I was sure that I was prepared to meet with the investor, but I was wrong. The first two questions rendered me speechless.

The investor wanted to see my cash flow projections. This is critical to an investor, since they want to know how long you will require their money to remain "invested" in your business.

Then, he stated simply, "I don't see the point of ROI on these documents." I did not realize ROI meant "return on investment." I knew I was going to work hard, and I was a good investment since the business was going to make money. However, this knowledge and a few quarters will still not buy a cup of coffee or interest an investor.

After a brief period of intense hesitation during which I smiled a lot, I stated that the budget would be surpassed by sales within six months and the business would be showing a profit at that time. He politely responded, "The date the budget is less than the sales figure is in six months . . . which is not that great. However, my question is when will I see a return on my investment?"

After a few moments of silence, I politely pointed to the break-even point on the budgets. The budgets included all expenses and my planned salary since I was going to be working full time in the business. I trusted the budgets were complete, but they were not.

Since I was not sure if the investors were going to invest, I did not insert into my budget the amount of money I was requesting from the investors. Therefore, the investor was not able to see how the business would benefit from the investment, take care of the indebtedness developed by the investment, and pay the investors back with interest. The budget was just paper since it did not include facts the investor required!

The investor was requesting the option regarding how the business would be conducted and how the dividends or payments would be made while the business was developing and until the capital investment in the business was paid back to the investors. I had studied for hours to be sure I knew the facts—how the cash flow projections were calculated and when we were going to meet and surpass the budget, which was going to be as quickly as possible—but these facts were only a small part of the equation. I needed to insert the investor funding balance into the budget and include the figures in the carry-over calculations each month before proceeding with my request.

As you can tell, I was prepared. However, I was still lost in the process!

The lessons I learned during the first minutes of the appointment were very valuable: prepare to discuss all the advantages and disadvantages during the start-up or expansion phase of your business, including specific facts regarding the cash flow and profit plan projections.

Financial Plan: Description of the Financial Structure

Personal Financial Statement

Determine the net worth of the owner, team leaders, and division or department leaders. It is important to prepare a comprehensive financial statement of the assets and liabilities of the owner and partners.

Assets

Often key assets are not included due to thinking about monthly obligations rather than full-term balances, so be sure to provide the accurate inventory and value of all assets, the equity amount from each investment, especially land or improved real estate, and the cash value of your life insurance policy. The value of the personal financial statement is based upon the assets and income accounts and "cash" versus term insurance policies, etc.

Liabilities

Paying off indebtedness is the key to reducing the liabilities and increasing net worth. If you are paying an extra principle payment each month, quarterly or annually, be sure to list all your efforts to reduce debt.

Once the facts, the picture of your financial status, is in front of you, take a moment to prepare a couple of statements to describe your status and future plans to reduce indebtedness and improve net worth.

Business Financial Statement

Begin the process for the business financial statement.

Assets

Once you have compiled the list of assets, include those things you can do to improve the value of the business's assets.

Liabilities

What can you do to improve the level of indebtedness? Can you establish a new strategic alliance with a vendor to reduce accounts or notes payable?

INDIVIDUAL FINANCIAL STATEMENT

Name: _____ SS# _ _ _ - _ _ - _ _ _ _

Address: _____ DL# _____

City: _____ State: _____ Zip: _____ Phone: _____

E-mail: _____ Cell Phone: _____

ASSETS
Bank: _____ Checking: $_____
                                   Savings: $_____
                         CD/Money Market: $_____
Real Estate: Valuation: $_____
                                 Property: $_____
Life Insurance: $_____
Accounts Receivable: $_____
                                            $_____
Personal Assets: $_____
Business Assets: $_____

                    TOTAL ASSETS: $_____

LIABILITIES
Notes Payable: _____
  Company: _____ Account: $_____
  Company: _____ Account: $_____
  Company: _____ Account: $_____
  Company: _____ Account: $_____
Accounts Payable: $_____
Outstanding Taxes: $_____

              TOTAL LIABILITIES: $_____

                    NET WORTH: $_____

Additional Facts: _____

Note: _____

BUSINESS FINANCIAL STATEMENT

Name: _____ Employer ID # _____

Address: _____

City: _____ State: _____ Zip: _____ Phone: _____

E-mail: _____ Web Site: _____

ASSETS

Bank: _____ Checking: $ _____

Savings: $ _____

Real Estate: Valuation: $ _____

Life Insurance of Key Executives: $ _____

Accounts Receivable: $ _____

                                        $ _____

Autos/Vehicles: $ _____

                                        $ _____

Business Assets in Depreciation Cycle: $ _____

Business Assets Valuation: $ _____

                TOTAL ASSETS: $ _____

LIABILITIES

Notes Payable:

                                        $ _____

                                        $ _____

                                        $ _____

                                        $ _____

Accounts Payable: $ _____

Outstanding Taxes: $ _____

            TOTAL LIABILITIES: $ _____

                NET WORTH: $ _____

Additional Facts: _____

Note: _____

At the end of the statement, you have a great opportunity to provide additional facts. Perhaps a unique situation is occurring this month and you will be resolving it in the near future. Whatever the unique facts are as of this "snapshot" view of your business, explain them in the Additional Facts section of the statement.

The section identified as Note includes the statement about your financial condition that is not reflected on the page yet.

A CPA typically provides a specific note at the end of the audited report. This statement is your chance to state the planned improvements to the current financial condition, so the person viewing the facts will realize what you are doing about the financial status. The note is a statement about what is not yet included within the snapshot of your personal or business financial statement.

Budget (Monthly, Quarterly, & Annual)

Complete budgets for a monthly, quarterly, and annual basis. Budgets should include best case, medium level, and worst case options. It is important to review all levels of business development so that you are sure the costs to provide the products/services in the marketplace will be paid and cover your costs to carry the inventory while you continue the business and reach the break-even point and beyond.

Creating a budget involves balancing your income against your expected expenses. Plan a revenue stream for each expense line. For ten expense lines, plan ten or more revenue streams for income.

Income
List each source of income:
Loans/Capital/Share or Stock Investments

Each gift or bonus
Each source of salary
Each source of contribution
Each planned sales/fundraising event
Vacation/Sick funds (plan for each, setting aside from income)

Expenses
List all expenses related to housing your business:
    lease or purchase price
    mortgage, indebtedness, interest, etc.
    insurance
    taxes
    maintenance and upkeep
List all vehicle costs/expenses:
    Department of Motor Vehicles fees
    lease or interest
    insurance
    maintenance, including gas, tires, brakes, and especially
      non-warranty items
List all equipment costs/expenses:
    purchase price
    maintenance
List all business expenses, supplies, and related costs.
    (It is important to keep this list tight and under review, because a miscellaneous expenses category can become a catch-all category and costs will tend to increase. Outlining specific office expense categories will help you control the budget.)
List all loans, leases, capital investment (ROI) payments.

BUDGET

Jan. Feb. Mar. Apr. May June July Aug. Sept. Oct. Nov. Dec.

Income (revenue streams)

Challenge: create one for each expense line!

1. Income
2. Income
3. Income
4. Income
5. Contribution (from sources)
6. Contribution (planned contributions from the business)
7. Gift
8. Bonus (anticipated or available to grant)
9. Salary (of owners and family members)
10. Salary
11. Salary
12. Capital Investment

Vacation budget, based upon policy

Planned sick or leave funds, based upon policy

Expense

13. Home (for sole-proprietor and if home equity is a business asset)
14. Maintenance
15. Office purchase/lease
16. Maintenance
17. Direct Labor
18. Indirect Labor
19. Auto Warranty/Service (include all expenses)
20. Maintenance
21. Equipment Warranty/Service
22. Maintenance
23. Business Expenses
22. Business Supplies
25. Loans/Leases/Capital Investment (ROI) Payments
26. Taxes
27. Misc., or Petty Cash (keep misc. expenses as a controlled figure, rarely used)

Cash Flow

With the estimates of the budget plan in hand, you can begin to set forth a cash flow plan. Once you know the requirements for cash to keep the business open and expanding, you can establish an effective marketing and sales plan to exceed the required income for the business.

CASH FLOW PLAN

Cash Flow IN
Month Total 5th 10th 15th 20th 25th Total at Month's End

Cash Flow OUT
Month Total 5th 10th 15th 20th 25th Total at Month's End

Monthly Cash Flow Summary

Compare the monthly budget and cash flow plan to the actual monthly budget and cash flow report, and review the business financial structure. Review and adjust the operational or marketing plan so the overall picture, the snapshot of your business progress, will continue to improve each month.

CASH FLOW ANALYSIS

	Jan.	Feb.	Mar.	Apr.	May	June	July	Aug.	Sept.	Oct.	Nov.	Dec.

Income
Sales Booked
Receivables
Other Income

Total

Expenses
Supplies Required

Direct Labor
Production Expenses
Marketing and Sales Costs
Development Costs
Indirect Labor
Taxes
Capital Investment
Loans
Leases

Total

Cash Flow

Total (+/- carry over from month to month; Goal: +/month!)

The only way to develop a cash flow system is to establish a structure that supports the flow of income and expenses. If you have a "heavy" week during the month, the business can "choke" based upon the progress or lack of sales in one week. The goal is to spread expenses evenly, week to week through the month.

Overhead expenses become the main conversation of business leaders until the break-even point is reached. Each and every month, the overhead expenses will be the focus until the business income surpasses expenses. The structure that supports profitability is the cash flow plan.

After you have prepared your cash flow plan, determine how you can enhance the cash flow. The following are some steps that will help you review and improve your cash flow.

1. List the income sources and expenses within the budget form.
2. Average the estimated income for the business for each date.

3. Review the due date of each of the main accounts/ and move the payment dates of accounts/ expenses that overload one of the payment dates. Insurance policy dates and lease/loan dates can be moved by the lender, so place the call and make the request to move the payments so that the weekly list of expenses is evenly distributed week to week.

4. Recheck the income/expense summary to be sure the average estimate payment for accounts/expenses is similar for each of the payment dates so the structure will support the flow of cash in and out of your business.

Planning Strategies

Monthly Plan
Set a monthly plan that contributes to your life, business, and community.

Personal/Family/Business Goal: $ _____

Vacation, Event, or Future Plans: + $_____

Contribution to:_____ $_____

Personal/Family/Business: $_____

Monthly Budget: $_____

Special Event, Personal Fund: $_____

Business Fund: $_____

The first mistake in establishing the business is spending every dime on the business and not planning a vacation. If you do not plan a vacation fund and take an annual vacation, plan a weekend getaway during the month. You may not get out of town each month, and you may not have a big budget to spend each month, but it is important to pull away from the daily business schedule to keep an objective view regarding the business. So, do yourself a favor; schedule some events of interest during the month and participate in activities that are not related to your business.

To keep the planned income, typical expenses, and financial goals in perspective, keep a monthly calendar available at all times. Write the facts on each date.

Quarterly and Annual Plan

To keep the planned income, typical expenses, and financial goals in perspective, keep a quarterly and annual plan available at all times. In your business, the quarterly report may not be based upon calendar quarters. So feel free to establish the format that works best for your financial and business evaluation dates.

Sun	*Mon*	*Tue*	*Wed*	*Thu*	*Fri*	*Sat*
	1	2	3	4	5 Income Expenses	6
7	8	9	10 Income Expenses	11	12	13
14	15 Income Expenses	16	17	18	19	20 Income Expenses
21	22	23	24	25 Income Expenses	26	27
28	29	30				

QUARTERLY CALENDAR

Specifics per week/month:

January

S	M	T	W	T	F	S	
	1	2	3	4	5	6	_____
7	8	9	10	11	12	13	_____
14	15	16	17	18	19	20	_____
21	22	23	24	25	26	27	_____
28	29	30	31				_____

February

S	M	T	W	T	F	S	
				1	2	3	_____
4	5	6	7	8	9	10	_____
11	12	13	14	15	16	17	_____
18	19	20	21	22	23	24	_____
25	26	27	28				_____

March

S	M	T	W	T	F	S	
				1	2	3	_____
4	5	6	7	8	9	10	_____
11	12	13	14	15	16	17	_____
18	19	20	21	22	23	24	_____
25	26	27	28	29	30	31	_____

Monthly, Quarterly, or Annually

It is important to keep future plans immediately in front of you and easy to access so that you can add notes frequently about any concerns or industry trends, or regarding any seasonal or other restrictions you might experience in obtaining specific production supplies, etc., at any particular time of year.

Contingencies

What are your contingency plans if sales do not meet projections at a particular time during the year? Does your industry conduct a specific sale or price reduction plan during a specific period of the year? Have you considered this fact? Do you have a plan B to increase sales? If a key strategic alliance does not proceed per the agreement, do you have a secondary plan to obtain the products/services required? Now is the time to consider your options should unexpected situations arise.

100 Percent Responsibility and Accountability

To be the leader, you have to be willing to take risks and adjust the plan when you are facing risks! Become the expert in charge of your plan and your finances. Do not leave the "money" or decision-making process to anyone else. To lead the team, division, or business you need to know the truth, the facts about the income and expenses in your life and your business.

Involving an accountant to prepare the financial reports and taxes for the business is advisable; however, you have to be the one who knows the numbers for your team, division, or business. To plan improvements, you have to know where you are, how you got there, and what you need to do to improve the status quo, especially when encountering unexpected difficulties.

Income Summary

With the monthly estimates in hand, prepare an annual summary to view the flow of income through the business and analyze to what extent it meets the needs of the owner, the team, partners, staff, and the business.

The business financial needs should be able to stand alone from your life plan. The mistake I made with my first corporation, when I used personal credit and resources to keep the business expenses handled, became a bad financial decision that grew worse each month. The company was growing so fast, the costs increased significantly, so I decided not to take a salary in an effort to offset the growing expenses. In addition, I used my credit cards to continue to develop the business. This is not a good decision for an established business or a good direction for a start-up or expanding business. The business needs to stand alone and cover the costs for growth and development. When you keep the financial status independent and healthy, the business will develop on merits it earns, based upon the established business financial structure.

Profit Plan: Description of the Profit Structure and Plans

With the monthly and annual financial summaries complete, take a moment to view the cash flow status of business from month to month. Analyze the availability of business funds from the profit perspective. Be sure you can set aside the profit margin each month to further develop the growth plans of the business as a part of the profit structure.

PROFIT PLAN

Actual Profit - Budgeted Profit = +/- Difference

_____ - _____ = +/- _____

A secret regarding improving the status quo: As soon as you focus on the numbers, the current status will improve. So, share the monthly plan and projections with each team member and employee involved. Make sure the numbers are openly displayed, visible to each key employee of the business, and included in each cost savings plan.

Building Your Seven Step Business Plan

7. Financial and Profit Plans

   A. Financial Plan (financial statements attached):

   B. Profit Plan:

Your Seven Step Business Plan

Planning is the key to success and profitability. Congratulations! You have accomplished the task. You are ready to insert each of the seven steps into your business plan!

Seven Step Business Plan

1. Structure
   A. Business Type:
   B. Industry:
   C. Legal Status (Corp., LLC, etc., and either C or S, etc.):

2. Placement
   A. Top Competitors:
      1.
      2.
      3.

B. Image Within the Industry:

3. Leadership
   A. Leader. Always a leader or trained to lead
      (BIO attached)?
   B. Strengths. Each leader BIO (attached):

4. Highlights and Purpose
   A. Purpose Statement:
   B. Highlights:

Owner(s)_____   Business_____
Address_____   Address_____
City_____ State__Zip__   City _____State__Zip__
License_____   Permit _____
Phone_____   Phone_____
Fax_____   Fax _____
Cell_____   Cell _____
E-mail _____   Web site_____
Insurance_____   Insurance _____

5. Vision and Mission Statement
   A. Vision Statement:
   B. Mission Statement:

1.   2.

3.   4.

5.   6.

7.   8.

9.   10.

11.   12.

Sound Bite (15 seconds):

6. Operational and Marketing Plans.
    A. Operational Plan:
    B. Marketing Plan:

7. Financial and Profit Plans
    A. Financial Plan (financial statements attached):
    B. Profit Plan:

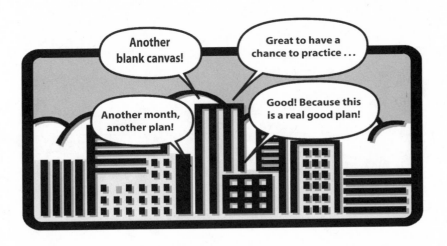

Seven Step Business Plan

Owner(s) _____ Business _____
Address _____ Address _____
City _____ State _____ Zip _____ City _____ State _____ Zip _____
License _____ Permit _____
Phone _____ Phone _____
Fax _____ Fax _____
Cell _____ Cell _____
E-mail _____ Web site _____
Insurance _____ Insurance _____

1. Structure
   A. Business Type: _____
   B. Industry: _____
   C. Legal Status (Corp., LLC, etc.) _____

2. Placement.
   A. Top Competitors: 1. _____ 2. _____ 3. _____
   B. Image Within the Industry: _____

3. Leadership.
   A. Leader. Always a leader or trained to lead (BIO attached)? _____
   B. Strengths. Each leader BIO (attached): _____

4. Purpose and Highlights.
   A. Purpose Statement: _____
   B. Highlights: _____

5. Vision and Mission Statements.
   A. Vision Statement: _____
   B. Mission Statement:
      1. _____   7. _____
      2. _____   8. _____
      3. _____   9. _____
      4. _____   10. _____
      5. _____   11. _____
      6. _____   12. _____

   Sound Bite (15 seconds): _____

6. Operational and Marketing Plans.
   A. Operational Plan: _____
   B. Marketing Plan: _____

7. Financial and Profit Plans.
   A. Financial Plan (financial statements attached): _____
   B. Profit Plan: _____

Notes: